The Lucrative Photographer

How To Become Indispensable
To Your Clients, Maximize Your Profitability,
And Regain Your Personal Life!

Mark D. Till

Second Edition

Till, Mark D.
The Lucrative Photographer: How To Become Indispensable To Your Clients, Maximize Your Profitability, And Regain Your Personal Life! by Mark D. Till, Cr.Photog.

Library of Congress Catalog Card Number: 00-90323

ISBN 0-9677918-0-4

Printed in USA

To purchase additional books and other educational material, please write to Mark Till Consulting, Six Surrey Lane, Natick, Massachusetts, 01760-3335, 508-655-9595, www.marktill.com.

DEDICATION

A book such as this is not possible without the help of friends and colleagues. I particularly want to thank my friend Carol for her tireless editing and proof reading, my cousin Christine for designing the book cover, and all my friends and colleagues who contributed their advice and guidance. A special thanks to Horace and Yvonne Holmes, who keep me centered on what is truly important—family.

Most of all I want to thank my wife Laura for her love, support, and patience. I couldn't have done it without you.

Thanks,

Mark

Table of Contents

Table of Contents

The Lucrative Photographer

Table of Contents

The Lucrative Photographer

Table of Contents

The Lucrative Photographer

Table of Contents

The Lucrative Photographer

Introduction

A BOOK FROM AN UNLIKELY SOURCE

If someone told me in college I would be writing a book, I most likely would have laughed in his or her face. I am someone who spent his entire college (and professional) career avoiding anything that had to do with writing (and reading for that matter). It is not that I couldn't write, it was because writing was not easy for me to do. Yet, here I am today an author of a book, and I have to admit, I have an enormous sense of accomplishment. Not bad for someone who once scored only 370 on the verbal part of his SATs.

The Lucrative Photographer is the result of over 20 years of personal experience and observations. I graduated from Babson College, in Wellesley, Massachusetts, in 1980 with a degree in Business Administration. I spent most of the next 10 years in Audit and Risk Management in banks throughout New England. In-between, I spent over two years as a financial planner, specializing in the needs of small business owners. In 1990, I opened Till Photography, after the FDIC closed the bank I worked for.

You may be wondering how I went from banking to photography. Like most of you I loved taking photographs. I worked as a photographer for my college yearbook where my claim to fame was photographing the 1980 Russian Figure Skating team that practiced at Babson prior to going to the Olympics at Lake Placid. After college, I began my "professional" photographic career by photographing a former girlfriend's wedding (a story for a book on its own). When the bank I was working for failed, I was already working as a photographer's assistant. So the leap into photography is not as far fetched as one might suspect.

However, from the beginning, the logic behind how photographers ran their businesses escaped me. I went from an environment where everything had a budget and a business plan to an industry where this concept was virtually unheard of. I was also surprised at the lack of industry data that was available on photography. Most industries have what is referred to as benchmark statistics on how their industry operates. In other words, minimum guidelines for what are considered a successfully run business. Without this type of data available, each photographer is left to "reinvent" the business wheel for his or her own self. Not surprisingly, most photographers' businesses are not run as well as they could be, and photographers, as a group, are poorly paid for their time and skill.

It was this lack of industry data that motivated me to develop my *Survey on Photographers' Business Practices*™. This survey was the first of its kind to be attempted in quite some time, and according to industry professionals, one of the most comprehensive surveys ever done. To participate in the survey and order a copy of the results, visit my website at http://www.marktill.com.

The survey confirmed what many of us in the business had thought all along: most studios try to be everything to everyone without having a clear business

Introduction

focus. Photographers don't have enough time to do what they want to do and also have a personal life. Most studios lack a formal business/marketing plan to give their business a sense of direction and purpose. And finally, most photographers don't have the necessary knowledge and skills to develop a lucrative price structure that will generate a respectable income for themselves and their families.

Being a lucrative photographer is more than just about being profitable. Over the years I have read and listened to many people talk about the various ways I could improve my photography, and make more money. However, oftentimes what was lacking was balance. That is why the first section of my book is entitled: Mind, Body, and Spirit. I interviewed several fellow photographers who not only have very lucrative businesses, but also take time out to spend time with their family and community. The older I get, the more important it is for me to spend time with family and friends. Life is short, and it is important for each of us to spend our time wisely.

This book is dedicated to changing the way photographers view themselves and their businesses. I hope you find this book to be a valuable resource that will help you obtain not only your professional goals but your personal ones as well.

The Lucrative Photographer

LUCRATIVE BUSINESS PRACTICES

Do you ever wonder why some photographers make lots of money while others; equally qualified always seem to struggle? I decided to do some research to find out for myself if there were some "secrets" certain photographers know that others do not.

I asked photographers around the U.S. and Canada ten questions related to how they operate their business to determine what, if anything, distinguishes those that succeed from all the rest. The ten questions were[1]:

1. Do you have a written marketing/business plan in place (with specific goals and dates for completion) that has been updated **within the past 12 months?**
2. Do you have a Unique Selling Proposition (USP) that explains **why prospects should do business with you,** as compared to all the other qualified businesses in your marketplace?
3. Do you spend at **least one-hour each day** on education and self-improvement?
4. Do you know how to recognize and capitalize on the **lifetime value** of your clients?
5. Do you spend at **least 50% of your business working hours** generating income? (Or is your day pre-occupied with administrative busy work?)
6. Are you optimistic about your personal and professional future?
7. Do you have a budget and cash management system to **adequately plan for current and future needs** (equipment, retirement, etc.)?

---

[1] The ten questions are a subset of my Lucrative Photographers Report Card. For a complete listing of the questions visit www.marktill.com/reportcard.html

8. Do you know your company's **break-even sales level** (both in total and by product line)?
9. Do you have a plan to address and resolve the most common quality and customer service problems that arise?
10. Do you regularly spend **the amount of time you would like** with your family and friends?

The results of the survey were startling. Photographers who answered yes to six or more questions <u>on average grossed 78% more in sales and 133% more in net income</u> as compared to those who answered yes to five or less. The average number of "yes" answers was 4.5.

I discovered that there was an inverse relationship between yes and no answers; the least likely someone was to answer yes to a question, the greater the impact that question had on their sales/income and vice versa.

QUESTIONS *LEAST LIKELY* TO BE ANSWERED, YES
#8 (21%) "Calculate break-even"
#1 (24%) "Written Business Plan"
#5 (28%) "50% or more of time is productive"

SUMMARY

This ten-question survey is not meant to be the definitive measure of what makes one studio succeed and another fail. However, it does point out several business practices that can dramatically improve your bottom line.

Throughout this book I will explore, in detail, the impact these ten questions have on your business and strategies you can use to implement them.[2]

---

[2] FREE Monthly Business Tips are available via email. Visit www.marktill.com and complete the guest registration page.

Introduction

Management by Dhamma

☞ What is Dhamma
☞ Creating A Balance Between Your Personal And Professional Lives
☞ Education And Self-Improvement
☞ Using Social Consciousness To Improve Your Community And Your Bottom Line

What is Dhamma?

In the spring of 1999 my local Chamber of Commerce conducted a seminar on spirituality in business. Interestingly enough it was one of the most heavily attended seminars the Chamber had run in years. One of the speakers was a gentleman named Sushil Bhatia, who is President of JMD Manufacturing in Framingham, Massachusetts.

Sushil runs his company using the concept: *Management By "Dhamma."* Dhamma is a Sanskrit word which means purpose in life, integrity, or doing the right thing for success. Sushil believes success is a journey, not a destination. It is the ability to fulfill your desires with ease, with enjoyment, and does not have to be at the cost of others. Success includes good health, energy, enthusiasm for life, creative freedom, emotional and psychological stability, and a sense of well-being and peace of mind. Dhamma is the performance of one's duty, appropriate to the situation, as an individual and as a member of society. To manage our lives, first and foremost is to stay healthy; physically, emotionally, and mentally.

I wanted to relate this story to you because I believe that to be truly lucrative is to have balance in one's own life. Hindu philosophy talks about the three roads to spirituality: The *Path of Yoga and Meditation*, the *Path of Duty*, and the *Path of Love*. Yoga is the study of harmony—of the mind, body, and life force (breathing). Each supports the other; none can exist without the other. How you implement this philosophy

2

is your choice. The important thing to remember is balance.

Creating a Balance Between Your Personal and Professional Lives

Without balance in one's life, professional accomplishments have little value. The purpose of this section is to remind each of us (myself included) that being lucrative is more than just about making money, it's about enjoying the voyage along the way.

If someone asked me when I opened my studio to list what I thought as important in being a lucrative photographer, I probably would not have included having a balance between my personal and professional lives. I was too obsessed with learning how to take better images and generating clients. Unfortunately, the same can be said for many business owners and particularly photographers. For many in our profession, photography isn't what they do; it's who they are. When you combine this with the fact that most photographers struggle to make a living, there is little time left for much else. In fact, 73% of those responding to my survey listed "lack of time" as their biggest obstacle.

A HARD LESSON TO LEARN

The need to balance one's personal and professional lives is a lesson most of us learn the hard way. In building our photography business, my wife and I worked 50+ hours each week with little time left over for family, friends, or each other. As far as I can remember, going back to college and high school, I have always worked long hours. First, it was because I needed to save money to go to college, then it was to pay for college once I got there. At some point in time working long hours just became a habit. The problem with constantly working is I forgot how to relax. After all, who has time to relax when there is so much that needs to get done?

My attitude started to change once I reached 40. Call it a mid-life crisis, but to me it was a wake-up call. Laura and I realized we had created a lifestyle we no longer wanted. We had no time for family, no time for fun and games, and my cholesterol was nearing stratospheric levels. We've recently spent more time with Laura's Dad, reacquainted ourselves with cousins and friends we hadn't seen in years, and have made going to the health club a priority. I feel like a new person.

I am writing this section of the book as much for myself as for you. Because the pace of life is constantly moving faster and faster, every now and then each of us needs to be reminded to slow down and remember why we do what we do.

Remember, *Management by Dhamma* includes good health, energy, enthusiasm for life, creative freedom, emotional and psychological stability, a sense of well-being, and peace of mind.

ARE YOU HAPPY WITH HOW YOU ARE CURRENTLY SPENDING YOUR TIME?

Even before you decide on your business niche, you need to decide what you want from life and choose a professional path that will help you achieve your personal goals, not the other way around.

One of my favorite authors and lecturers, Tom Winninger, likes to tell the story of Alice in Wonderland and in particular the part where Alice meets the Cheshire cat. As the story goes, Alice comes to a crossroad and can't decide which path to take. She sees the cat in the tree and stops to ask directions. The cat asks her, "Where do you want to go?" Alice replies, "I'm not sure." To which the cat responds, "Well then any road will get you there."

The story raises an interesting question: Where do you want to go? Not just professionally, but personally as well. If your goal is to spend more time with your kids on the weekends, being a wedding photographer may be last thing you want to do. The more successful (busy) you get, the farther away you get from your attaining your personal goal. Just like a business plan, you need to know where you are today and where you want to be in the future.

GETTING STARTED

Kirsten Snow is our New England Art Leather/GNP representative and is one of the most positive and uplifting people I have ever met. Even when she has had every right to complain, she never does. When I told her I wanted to include a section in my book on having balance between personal and professional lives she was thrilled. Kirsten firmly believes that creating balance in one's life can create even more success. "Becoming a better person translates into your success as a business owner," says Kirsten.

The Lucrative Photographer

Kirsten suggests you start by looking at *how you are currently spending your time* as compared to *how you would like to spend your time*. The chart below will help you complete this exercise. While there is no right or wrong answer, you may be surprised at how wide a gap you have between where you are today and where you want to be tomorrow.

HOW ARE YOU SPENDING YOUR TIME?		
Activity	% of Time Current	% of Time Ideal
Work		
Education		
Vacation		
Hobby		
Family and Friends		
Exercise		
Personal Time		
Other		
Total	100%	100%

The next step is to write down what is important to you *personally* as well as *professionally*. Assuming financial success, list the personal goals you would like to accomplish. For example, maybe it is to learn to play the piano, or paint, or even write a book.

Once you make your list, assess whether your current lifestyle and career track is moving you closer or farther away from your goals. If you are on the right track, great! If not, think of what changes you would like to make. In part, completing this exercise helped me realize I wanted to change career paths. As with your business, it is a good idea to sit down each year and assess where you are, where you are going, and where you want to be.

PERSONAL AND PROFESSIONAL GOALS

Personal Goals _____

_____

_____

_____

Professional Goals _____

_____

_____

_____

HAVE A LIFE OUTSIDE OF PHOTOGRAPHY

In preparing for this section of the book, I decided to interview other photographers who seem to have created a good balance between work and photography. One couple that always seems to have their priorities straight is Horace and Yvonne Holmes. Laura and I sat down with Horace and Yvonne to ask them what they do to keep well balanced.

First is where they stay when they travel. They make it a point to stay at a facility (whenever possible) that has a health club. I can attest that I have seen both of them at the health club when we have traveled to the same conference.

They also close their studio for lunch each day. I happened to call them one day and got their voice mail message and thought it was a great idea. Even if it's just for a half-hour, shut the phone off and enjoy a few bites in peace.

While we're on the subject of time off, Horace and Yvonne don't work on Sundays because that is their church day. They also don't work on Monday so they can do personal errands. They believe that success is more than just about dollars; it is also about balance.

As a husband and wife in business they understand the importance of trying to take care of one another. They take an interest in each other's interests, so later in life when they retire, they will still have something to talk other about. They also try to incorporate their family into everything they do.

It is very refreshing and inspiring to listen to Horace and Yvonne. They have managed to build a very lucrative business without sacrificing their quality of life.

Another couple that is well grounded is Julia Russell and Jay Goldsmith of Portsmouth, New Hampshire. Julia photographs exclusively weddings and Jay, environmental family portraits. What I find appealing is their schedule. Jay works only May through October and Julia limits the number of weddings she photographs to 22-25 per year.

In the off-season Jay works on "personal" photographic projects completely different from his family portraits. He also enjoys woodworking. Both like to travel and do so extensively during their winter hiatus.

Every so often it is important to look at how you are spending your time. It may be time to make a few changes.

SET ASIDE TIME FOR THINGS
THAT ARE PERSONALLY IMPORTANT TO YOU

Laura and I made a decision that we wanted to spend more time together away from work. Our solution was to have a "date" every Wednesday for lunch. I pick her up at work and we go out to lunch. I have to say it's been great! Even though it's only an hour, the time together is very important to us. We don't talk about work (or at least we try not to), we just get together to spend time with each other. With our busy life style we needed to make it part of our schedule. The same is true for exercise. I have set aside a certain portion of each day (first thing in the morning) and I go to the health club to workout.

In both instances, I blocked out time in my day for something that is personally important to me. If for some reason something comes up that can't be changed, I reschedule the event to another time. It was once said to me that what we spend our time doing in the long run is what is truly important to us. How are you spending your time?

SUMMARY

This section is not meant to be a sermon or to profess one philosophy over another. Rather it is a challenge for each of us to reflect on what is truly important to us. To understand that while professional success is important, it is only a part of who we are. How we spend our time, in the long run, defines who we are and what we hold to be important. Each of us needs to go down the path that will take us to where we want to go.

One of the highest compliments you can bestow upon someone in the Jewish faith is to call that person a "mench"—a human being, a good person. I wish you all much success in your endeavors, but most of all I would like everyone to say you were not only professionally successful but also you were a mench as well.

Time (Performance) Management

Tom Winninger refers to Time Management as Performance Management, because as he points out, you can't really manage time, you can only spend it. There are always 60 seconds in a minute, 60 minutes in an hour, 24 hours in a day, etc. How you choose to spend your time is a key factor in your ultimate success.

One of the common threads of Time Management is prioritizing what needs to be done, performing those tasks that are important to the success of your goals, and minimizing people and tasks that distract from what you want to accomplish.

While I don't profess to be an expert in Time Management, I would like to share a few tips I have learned over the years.

HAVE A WRITTEN TO-DO LIST
Studies have shown that having written daily goals can double your *effective* output! I have to admit that I don't always write things down as I should, but when I do, I am always amazed at how much I get accomplished. Why then don't I write things down everyday? I get busy and caught up in the day-to-day rush of just getting it done. If you could *double your effective output,* is it worth spending a few minutes each day to create a to-do list? I think so, and I challenge each of you to prepare a to-do list (if you do not do so already) every day for the next two weeks. At the end of the two weeks review how much you accomplished.

If you have been faithful in completing and updating your to-do list, I'm sure you'll want to continue the habit. Of course a to-do list will not help if you don't look at it every so often. Make sure you check your list several times during the day.

"DO THE THINGS YOU DREAD FIRST, AND THE SATISFACTION OF DOING WHAT YOU ENJOY WILL BE EVEN GREATER."[3]

If you hate calling reception halls to get them to recommend you, do that first thing in the morning and reward yourself by doing something you like later on. When you don't like to do something it is easy to make excuses not to do it. Unfortunately, ignoring the task won't make it go away. Get it over quickly, you'll feel better after you've completed.

THE 80/20/80 RULE

We've all heard of the 80/20 rule, first coined by the Italian sociologist and economist, Vilfredo Pareto (1843-1923). The rule states that 80% the wealth comes from 20% of the population.[4] The same can be said from your customers—80% of your profits, come from just 20% of your customers. The reverse is also true—20% of your customers account for 80% of customer service issues.

---

[3] Personal Performance: Empowering Your Life and Your Career, Thomas J. Winninger, CSP, CPAE, ©1995, Winninger Resource Group.
[4] Customers That Count, Tony Cram, ©2001, Financial Times—Prentice Hall

The lesson is clear, invest 80% of your time your time and marketing efforts on the 20% of your customers who will generate 80% of your profits.[5]

KNOW WHERE THE TIME HAS GONE

When I worked as a Risk Manager, I had to account for every hour I worked because my time was billed to the departments with whom I consulted. I got into the habit of keeping a daily log of my activities. The log was quite humbling. Although I thought I was working hard all day, there were times when I wasn't as effective as I thought. In other words, I clowned around too much.

For the next four weeks keep track of how you are spending your time. You don't have to keep records minute-to-minute, half-hour segments are sufficient. Use your calendar or a pad of paper to track your activity. At the end of each day use the chart below to summarize your results.

At the end of the month, combine the daily results and look at where you spent your time. If you were honest, I'm sure there will be quite a few surprises.

After reviewing your results, ask yourself if you are spending your time doing what is most important to your business and to you personally. Are you performing tasks that should be delegated or outsourced? (Such as album and frame assembly.)

---

[5] *Customers That Count*, Tony Cram, ©2001, Financial Times—Prentice Hall

---

DAILY TIME TRACKING LOG

Date: _____

| | | Time |
Activity		Spent
_____		_____
_____		_____
_____		_____
_____		_____
_____		_____
_____		_____
_____		_____

I gave this assignment to one of my clients, who after reviewing the results, realized he was spending only 20% of his time actually generating income (photographing and marketing) the remaining 80% was consumed with day-to-day minutia, yet another example of the 80/20 rule.

The majority of your *working* time should be spent either photographing a client or thinking of and implementing ways to grow your business. If you are spending all of your time on routine day-to-day activities, there is no time left over for personal or professional growth.

At one time or another, each of us falls into the trap of trying to do it all ourselves. When Laura and I first started in the business, we worked frantically in the fall to get all the production done. We figured we'd catch up on household chores and the like in January or February. But it never happened. Something else came up and we got further behind. Being ever so optimistic, we figured we'd just work harder next year, and things would be different. We've since learned our lesson.

I once heard that the definition of insanity was doing the same thing over and over again but expecting a different result. If at the end of each week, month, or year, you are no better off than you were when you started, it is time to make some changes. Prioritize your goals and time with your personal values and happiness in mind. Look for ways to delegate less important tasks to staff or vendors.

INCREASE YOUR SALES BY $130,000

As I illustrated with my ten-question survey in the introduction, spending an additional one-hour each day behind the camera can result in an increase in sales of $130,000 or more. I mention this again because as photographers, we now have the opportunity to create some wonderful images "in-house." Products and services once available only through a lab or outside resource can now be done in-house. However, it is important to remember that survey respondents listed a lack of time as the biggest obstacle photographers face in running their business.

Before taking on a new task, remind yourself why you are doing what you do, and ask yourself if you would be better served by having someone else do it for you and concentrating on those activities that will make you money and help you reach your goals.

If you decide that you need to perform a digital function yourself, make sure you factor in your time in the price of the work you sell. For example, suppose you sell an image for $150 processed traditionally through your lab. If you need to spend a half-hour of time on Photoshop to complete the job and your time is worth $150 per hour, I would recommend you charge $225 for the image you are doing in-house. Why? Because you can either spend time behind the camera or in front of the computer, not both. If you want to do the work yourself, you will need to compensate yourself accordingly.

IMPORTANT VERSUS URGENT

A consistent theme repeated over and over by time management experts is handling items that are important versus items that are urgent. One of the best explanations I have heard comes from Tom Winninger. He related a theory put forth by President Dwight D. Eisenhower, which says "There Is An Inverse Relationship Between Things That Are Important And Things That Are Urgent." According to President Eisenhower's theory, the more important an item is the less urgent; the more urgent an item, the less important it is.[6]

The application of this theory is that items that are urgent, but not important are what prevent most of us from accomplishing our goals. If all we do is go from "fire to fire" we have no time left over for the really important tasks. Our goal is to spend most of our time on items that are important, but not urgent. Marketing

---

[6] Personal Performance: Empowering Your Life and Your Career, Thomas J. Winninger, CSP, CPAE, ©1995, Winninger Resource Group.

is a good example. Marketing is clearly important, but when you're busy, it doesn't seem urgent. After all, you have plenty to do. When things slow down however, marketing takes on a more urgent need. If, on the other hand, you spend time each day or week on marketing, it won't ever get to the urgent stage.

I also believe the more urgent an item is, the less options you have to resolve the issue. If you did not set aside money to fund your retirement, as you get older there are fewer and fewer option available to you to rectify the situation.

Go back and take a look at where you are spending your time. If you never seem to have the time to do the activities you need to do to grow your business, it may be time for you to add staff or outsource certain tasks before the important tasks become critically urgent.

ELIMINATE THINGS THAT CAUSE STRESS OR DRAIN ENERGY

Personal Coach and author Cheryl Richardson (*Take Control of Your Life*) has a simple but effective philosophy—"Eliminate it, do it, hire it, or chuck it."[7] Cheryl believes everything we do, think, and eat can have a positive or negative effect on our energy level. Unfortunately, according to her research, that suggests that most of us spend up to 75-80% of our time with negative energy activities. These activities include not exercising, poor dietary habits, not completing things on our to-do list, personal and professional relationships, etc.

---

[7] *Take Control Of Your Life*, Cheryl Richardson, ©1998 Broadway Press

The Lucrative Photographer

Cheryl's research supports what I stated earlier, that up to 80% of what we do is non-productive and takes away from what is truly important. By eliminating or at least minimizing energy-draining activities, we will lead happier and more productive lives.

When I first started in the business, I would re-number each negative after sorting through the proofs so people would have prints in numerical order. Although it took a lot of time, I thought it was something important to my clients. One day I asked a few clients if it was important and come to find out, it was not. Just because you have always done something doesn't mean it is really necessary. Look for tasks that you can eliminate.

There is an old saying, "Don't put off until tomorrow what you can do today." (An expression I don't use as nearly as I should.) Instead of putting something off (again) do it now, you'll have a sense of accomplishment and you'll feel better.

If there are tasks you can't get to or just don't enjoy doing, hire someone to do them for you. Album assembly is a task I never enjoyed. It took a lot of time and I found it boring. My solution: I have my album companies assemble my albums and I don't know how I survived doing it any other way. The same is true with masking negatives. I was one of the first studios in my area to use Proshots™. By masking the orders online I have dramatically reduced the time it takes to mask an order. Look for chores that can be done by someone else, and hire someone to do it. Save your time for things that are really important to you.

If you're like us, your basement and attic are full of things you haven't used in years. Set aside a few hours each month or one day once or twice each year and go through your files, drawers, boxes, and cabinets. If you have things that take up space and you haven't used them in six months or so, you probably never will, so get rid of them.

One of the reasons many of us are not able to get to the things we need to do is because our energy is being drained by negative energy activities. Medical studies have shown a link between positive thinking and good mental and physical health. Setting aside time for things that are important to you is an important part of that process. Once you rid yourself of things that are emotionally and physically distracting, you will be in a much better position to address the issues that will have a positive impact on your personal and professional lives.

Education And Self-Improvement

One of the most eye-opening statistics I have heard is that if you spend as little as *one hour each day* on improving your skills, knowledge of your industry and clients, you will be in the *top 5-10% in your field within 18 months!*[8] I find this statistic incredible for two reasons. First, that 90-95% of people in each industry spend so little time on self-improvement. If you spend only one hour out of 40 (one hour a week), you can be in the top 20% of your field in less than 12 months. In many ways it is not very surprising because most people spend their time going from fire to fire. They are so caught up in day-to-day minutia that they don't have any time for strategic thinking and self-improvement.

Second, I am amazed it takes only 12-18 months to overtake virtually all of your competitors just on the power of knowledge. When I first heard this statistic, I was a little skeptical. I began to look at the top photographers in the various specialty areas and noted that without exception, each of the photographers possessed superior knowledge of their particular style of photography. The same is true for the folks who always seem to be on the cutting edge of digital imaging. They didn't just stumble across their digital success; they have invested many hours of their time learning about the medium and how to apply it to their own studio situation. If you look at the photographers

---

[8] Personal Performance: Empowering Your Life and Your Career, Thomas J. Winninger, CSP, CPAE, ©1995, Winninger Resource Group.

who always seem to win the top honors at each convention, I will bet my last dollar that each of them constantly thinks of new poses to try or innovative ways to light a subject or simply practice. When was the last time you took a day off just to take photographs for yourself or to practice a new technique?

Even outside of photography, the top people in their industry are almost exclusively the ones who invest the most time improving their skills and knowledge. Michael Jordan, perhaps the greatest basketball player of all-time, was the first person on the court at practice and the last to leave. The same was true of Larry Bird. How many hours a week do you spend expanding your knowledge and improving your skills?

EDUCATION DOES NOT MEAN SPENDING LOTS OF MONEY ON SEMINARS AND CONVENTIONS

It can be as simple as reading trade journals or practicing new posing and lighting techniques. A great way to get started is to set aside one day a month just to photograph something, not for a client, but for you personally.

Another inexpensive idea is listening to educational tapes while you drive or exercise. While there are times I would rather listen to music, listening to the tapes helps motivate me and stimulates new ideas. Listening to the tapes while you exercise or drive is also an efficient use of your time (of course it is not a good idea if your spouse or family is in the car and they want to talk with you). The next time you are in your car or at the gym give educational tapes a try.

The next tip is to set aside a block of time each day for reading. Reading is one of those activities that is important but not urgent, and it has an intangible goal. The temptation is to put aside reading when there are things to do that have a more tangible deadline. This is one of the reasons why people don't spend the time to improve their knowledge. If self-improvement is important, you will make it a priority and schedule it into your day.

Of course seminars and conferences are great educational tools as well. I learn a lot from meeting with fellow photographers from around the country. Make it a priority to attend a seminar or regional school each year. But conferences are not free. Later, I will cover cash management tips to help you have the money you need for education (and other purposes), when you need it.

It is also important to expand your learning outside our industry (helps to think outside the box). Throughout this book I have made references to people outside our industry. If you want to learn about "time management" for instance, read whatever you can find on the subject from people who have created their own niche on the topic. Expanding your learning outside photography challenges you to grow and can keep you one step ahead of your competition.

Using Social Consciousness To Improve Your Community And Your Bottom Line

Although I can't point to any specific study, virtually every successful business owner I know gives something back to the community in which they work and live. It may be in the form of volunteering their time, donating their services, and of course, donating money.

I had the good fortune of chairing a seminar held by my local Chamber of Commerce on giving back to the community. Without exception, each speaker noted that being charitable was also good for his or her business! Each speaker could directly attribute additional business because of his or her charitable acts.

The results experienced by these owners are not unique. A 1994 survey conducted by Cone Communications (Boston) and Roper Research (New York) supports that being socially responsible is also good business.[9]

- 78% of adults said they were more likely to buy a product associated with a cause they care about

---

[9] *Double-Dip: How To Run A Value Lead Business And Make Money, Too.* Ben Cohen and Jerry Greenfield, Fireside, ©1997 Simon and Schuster.

- 66% of adults said they'd be more likely to switch brands to support a cause they care about
- 54% of adults said they'd pay more for a product that supports a cause they care about
- After price and quality, 33% consider a company's business practices the most important factor in deciding whether or not to buy a brand

CIRCLE OF GIVING

Kirsten Snow first introduced me to the concept of the *Circle Of Giving*. Kirsten explained it to me this way: "The more you give, the more you get back in return. Acts of kindness have a way of coming back to you, not always directly and in ways you least expect. It also builds a sense that you come from a place of plenty (that you have an abundance of what you need) versus a place of lack."

There is no couple that better illustrates the spirit of the *Circle Of Giving* than Horace and Yvonne Holmes of Macon, Georgia. Their charitable contributions are truly inspiring. They have established a mentoring program for photographers around the country, established a partnership with Canon and Kodak to help kids at risk learn to become photographers, and have taken portraits of kids to help place them in adopted homes, and so much more.

They have made a name for themselves by making a difference in their community. Horace and Yvonne's charitable acts are *not* motivated by self-interest, but they have been very good for business because of the publicity it generates.

Another example of a company committed to giving back to the community is Lasertone Corporation, in Wayland, Massachusetts. Lasertone remanufactures laser toner cartridges and has been one the area's fastest (and most profitable) companies. President and owner, Nancy Connolly remarked that the "movers and shakers" in each community regularly attend charitable events. In addition, Nancy says these people tend to be what she refers to as "back of the book readers." That is they look at the back of the program book to see who did and did not contribute to the charity. Nancy attributes part of her company's success to her charitable activities. When she calls on these people, they remember seeing Lasertone's name, and it has allowed her to get a foot in their door. Her point is that you need to know who your target audience is and what causes are important to them, because you may want to make their causes important to you.

WHERE TO BEGIN

We often read in the paper or watch on TV a celebrity promoting a cause to help a friend or for some personal reasons. A good place to start is to look for a cause that you have a personal or professional connection to. If you photograph children, you could support charities such as the March of Dimes or the Jimmy Fund. Look for opportunities to contribute to the local causes in your community.

Among the many ways to contribute: donating your services at a charity auction, offering a promotion in which the sitting fee or a portion of the proceeds will be donated to a charity of your client's choice, or volunteering your time. You can even team up with other photographers. I was contacted by the Muscular Dystrophy Association for an event in which I was to be "arrested" and had to call my friends to raise bail. A fellow photographer was also contacted so we had a photograph taken of both of us at the event. The photograph and related story about both of us appeared in the local newspaper.

As anyone who has purchased a home knows, you must put a substantial down payment on the home while your mortgage application is being processed. The down payment is placed into an escrow account, which earns interest. Instead of keeping the interest from his real estate agency, this realtor discloses to the buyer and seller that the interest earned will be donated to a charity (in his case Muscular Dystrophy). This past year the interest totaled over $18,000! Which is also a nice tax deduction. Consider doing the same thing with interest earned from retainers from future weddings or social events.

One of my favorite ideas was donating stock. If you own shares of a stock or mutual fund that has seen significant appreciation, you may be able to donate some (or all) of the stock to a charity. Current tax laws allow you to deduct the full fair market value of the stock at the time of the charitable donation (if you have owned the stock for more than one year). For example, you bought a stock at $10 per share and it is now worth $50 per share. You are allowed to deduct the full $50 per share on your taxes as a charitable gift. On the flip side, if you own a stock that is valued below what you paid for it, you should sell the stock first, take the loss, and then make the donation. (Note: This is not intended as tax advice, if you have any specific tax questions you should seek the advice of a qualified tax professional).

WHY COMPANIES DONATE[10]

An article appearing in our local weekly newspaper reviewed the charitable activities of three of the largest companies in our town. While each company approached charitable donations differently, they all agreed that giving back to the community is about being a good neighbor.

Josh Ostroff of the Natick Education Foundation was quoted as saying; "I think that most companies acknowledge a connection between the health of the community and the success of their business. By supporting local community groups and causes, they're helping themselves."

From a financial standpoint, there are limited tax advantages, states, Jim Sowar, CPA with Arthur Anderson. He says, "You'd be hard-pressed to say they (companies) are donating for the tax benefit. The economics just don't work. It is mainly driven by doing good deeds."

---

[10] From *The Business of Charity*, ©June 15th, 2001, Natick Bulletin & Tab, By Micah Sachs, www.townonline.com

Do It For The Right Reasons

While being socially responsible can have a positive impact on your studio's bottom line, it should NOT be your primary goal for being charitable or supporting a cause. If this is your objective, you are doing it for the wrong reason, and it will eventually catch up to you. Your objective in giving back to your community should be made with altruistic intentions. Get involved because you believe in the cause. It's all right to get a little PR out of your activity, but that is an added benefit. The real reward is in the act of kindness itself. Or as Dr. Bob Shillman, CEO and President and Chairman of Cognex Corporation in Natick put it, "Without the work of good men, the world falls apart."

Resources

COMPANIES
JMD Manufacturing, Inc., Sushil Bhatia, President, 59 Fountain Street, Framingham, Massachusetts 01702, (508) 620-6563

Lasertone Corp., Nancy Connolly, President, 526 Boston Post Road, Wayland, Massachusetts, 01760, (508) 358-1200, www.lasertonecorp.com

Art Leather/GNP, Kirsten Snow, P.O. Box 157, Marshfield Hills, Massachusetts 02051-0157, (781) 829-9940. www.artleather.com and www.gnp.com

BOOKS
Take Time For Your Life, Cheryl Richardson, ©1998 Broadway Books. http://www.cherylrichardson.com/

The 7 Habits Of Highly Effective People, ©1990, Stephen R. Covey, Fireside Book, Simon and Schuster

Double-Dip: How To Run A Value Lead Business And Make Money, Too. Ben Cohen and Jerry Greenfield, Fireside, ©1997 Simon and Schuster.

AUDIO TAPES
Personal Performance, Empowering Your Life and Your Career, ©1995,Thomas J. Winninger, CSP, CPAE, Winninger Resource Group, (612) 896-1900

Become Indispensable To Your Clients

☞ Are You Unique?
☞ What Is A Niche?
☞ Do You Really Need To Specialize?
☞ Unique Selling Proposition
☞ Price is Rarely an Effective USP

Are You Unique?

If I were to ask you to give me a *single image* that "defines" your unique style and displayed it next to photographs from your fellow photographers, would *your target audience* be able to identify your work from that of your competitors? Based on my experience, probably not.

In the world of art, there is no mistaking a painting by Monet, Picasso, Rembrandt, or Georgia O'Keefe. Not only did each artist have a unique and distinctive style, they influenced and changed the way subsequent artists approached their craft. Even today, as photographers, we talk about using Rembrandt lighting and use Photoshop™ to create Monet-like effects.

While we like to think of our work as being unique, most of the images you create and products you offer are similar to those produced by your competitors. It is only natural for people who attend the same seminars, enter prints in the same competition, and read the same magazines, to have similar styles. Granted, some photographers are more skilled than others. However, when you compare photographers of comparable aptitude, the differences become less apparent. The distinction is even smaller if both photographers use the same lab, the same film, or album and frame manufacturer.

When there is parity of style and product, in order to differentiate yourself from the other qualified photographers in your area, you will *need to compete on something other than the uniqueness of your photographic style.*

HOW UNIQUE ARE YOU?

- Is your work worth paying a premium for?
- Is your work unique enough to make people change their plans to have you as their photographer?
- When people inquire about your services, are they more concerned about your availability than your price?
- Is your target audience's perception of your studio what YOU want it to be?
- Do you know who your target audience is and who they are not?
- Will you turn down business if it is NOT part of your specialty?

Take a moment or two to complete the above quiz. If you said yes to five or more questions—you're well on your way. If not, don't despair; help is a few pages away.

What Is A Niche?

Simply stated, a niche is a focused, specialized strategy aimed at a target market (audience) that has significantly different needs from the broader market.[11]

If we define "all types of photography" as the broadest market, than specializing in "wedding photography" would be an example of a segment of the market that has a need different from the population as a whole. However, wedding photography is still a broad category. Do you go after the carriage trade market or the mass market? Do you specialize in portraits or candids, color or black and white? I think you get the idea. A niche marketer does not try to be everything to everyone. They identify who their target audience is and who it is not, and focus all their marketing efforts towards that end.

A niche can also be defined as serving an untapped or under-served segment of the market:

Suppose you are looking to open a photography studio in your area. One studio already focuses on weddings, another on children, and a third on environmental family portraits. An untapped market may be pets or high school seniors. If the wedding photographer specializes in illustrative portraits, consider a photojournalistic approach. Another approach is to look at how the photographers are servicing their

---

[11] *Price Wars: How To Win The Battle For Your Customers*, Thomas J. Winninger, ©1994, St. Thomas Press.

clients. As we'll see later, it is easier to distinguish yourself with exceptional customer service than it is to distinguish yourself by offering an exceptional product.

One of the best examples of niche marketing is Las Vegas. Las Vegas has over 120,000 hotel rooms and has on average a 90% occupancy rate. This is truly amazing. There are dozens of casinos up and down "The Strip" each one offering virtually an identical product: *gambling, food, entertainment, and lodging.*

How does each of these casinos stay in business? By undercutting one another? No, they have succeeded by creating a theme park within the confines of their facility. In Las Vegas you can "visit" Rio, Paris, Venice, Bellagio, Ancient Rome, Ancient Egypt, and even go onto the bridge of the Starship Enterprise. Each casino has a target audience, whose needs are different from the population (Las Vegas) as a whole. By creating a niche; a unique, one-of-a-kind experience—they have all flourished.

Leonardo daVinci may be the best example of why it is important to have a niche and stay focused. An ad for an exhibit at the Boston Museum of Fine Arts dubbed daVinci as the world's most successful failure. He was a painter—the Mona Lisa is one of the most recognized and copied works of art in the world. He was also an inventor—he designed proto-types for both the helicopter and the airplane hundreds of years before they would be built. Yet he lived his life in poverty. daVinci had a reputation for genius but also for never completing what he started. For all of his accomplishments, he died a pauper. daVinci's life is a great lesson for all business owners and particularly photographers. Many photographers believe the quality of their work alone is enough to make people flock to their doors with open arms and wallets. Photographers also like to dabble. *"I like the variety of different types of photography"* is the mantra of many a photographer. daVinci possessed more talent than most of us could hope to have and no doubt, liked variety, but it took hundreds of years for his talents to be appreciated. If you don't mind the wait, by all means dabble. If you want to be lucrative today, create a niche.

Do You Really Need To Specialize?

For many of you, the very idea of specializing (limiting the type of photography you offer) may seem a bit crazy. It certainly goes against the conventional way of thinking prevalent in photography today—cradle to grave photographic coverage. So why then am I so insistent on the need to have a niche? A company with a well-defined niche is easier to manage, easier to promote, and most importantly, more lucrative. The benefits to limiting yourself to a single specialty can be summed up in the following categories:

- Competition
- Lack Of Time
- Brand-Loyalty
- The Specialist
- Unique Markets
- Confused Prospects Don't Buy (From You)
- Past Success Does Not Guarantee Future Success

Let's take a look at each one in greater detail beginning with Competition.

COMPETITION

You may be fortunate to live in an area where there literally is NO competition for your services. If so, enjoy it while it lasts. For the rest of us, competition is a way of life. As soon as there is at least one other company offering photographic services in your market area, there's competition. The need to create a niche increases with each new competitor.

Become Indispensable To Your Clients

Suppose there is more than one photographer in your area that photographs children. Why should someone choose photographer A over photographer B? Before you answer "quality" or "price", think about it. The cheapest photographer is not always the busiest and there are a lot of very talented photographers who are starving for business. There has to be a reason why clients are drawn to one studio over another. A well-defined niche can help you distinguish yourself from your competition by making you *indispensable* in the minds of your *ideal client*.

LACK OF TIME

Have you ever had the experience where you were intently working on a project only to be interrupted? How easy was it to go back to the original project after the interruption? It is very difficult to switch gears in midstream. As a result each project takes longer to complete than expected, your to-do list gets longer, your anxiety level rises, and your ability to concentrate weakens.

By comparison, when you focus on one subject, your mind will work overtime to solve the problem or reach your goal. You begin to think of new poses, new techniques, and new ways to promote your services. It's as if the floodgates of creativity have been opened.

As noted in my survey, one of the biggest challenges facing photographers is the lack of time to do everything they need and want to do. If you don't have enough time to complete your current tasks, it stands to reason that offering more products and services will only make matters worse. A highly focused niche saves the most precious resource of all, time.

BRAND-LOYALTY

Studies have shown that despite the availability of cheaper generic products, brand names account for over 90% of all purchases made, even though brand names cost up to 40% more than their generic counterparts[12]. Brand names carry with them a sense of quality and assurance. People also tend to associate the brand name with the product or service they offer. For example, which of the following do you use?

BRAND NAMES	
Kleenex™	facial tissue
Rollerblades™	in-line skates
Jacuzzi™	hot tub
Band-Aid™	plastic bandages
Scotch Tape™	cellophane tape
Q-Tips™	cotton swabs
Rollerblades™	in-line skates
JELLO™	Gelatin

In each of the above examples the brand name product has become synonymous with the generic product category.[13]

---

[12] *Selling The Invisible: A Field Guide To Modern Marketing*, Harry Beckwith, ©1997, Warner Books.

[13] *The Twenty-Two Immutable Laws of Branding*, Al Ries and Laura Ries, ©1998 Harper Business

Become Indispensable To Your Clients

The good news is, that once established, brand loyalty is hard to shake. The bad news is that creating a brand name takes time. It is easier to create a new brand name (niche) than it is to gain market share on a well-entrenched brand name. Could you name a competitor's brand name for any of the above products? Look for ways to service your market that are not being addressed by your competition. If your target market needs this service, you are on your way to creating your own USP and brand name.

THE SPECIALIST

If you have a problem, who do you want to fix it, someone who does a little of this and a little of that or someone who specializes in exactly what you need?

Public perception is that someone who specializes in one area of expertise must know more and is better qualified than someone who dabbles. Who do you think will earn a higher salary, a jack-of-all-trades, or a specialist? Remember daVinci.

Random House Dictionary defines a specialist and specialty as follows:

> *"**Specialist**—a person who devotes him/herself to one subject or to one particular branch of a subject or pursuit"*

> *"**Specialty**—an article with such strong consumer demand that it is <u>at least partially removed</u> from price competition"*

The Lucrative Photographer

It should come as no surprise that by definition; that to be a specialist, you need to *specialize* in one area of photography. What may surprise you is that the _definition of a specialty_ includes the diminishing importance of price to the consumer!

Not only is being a specialist easier for the public to understand, but also the buying public prefers to use a specialist and is often willing to pay a premium for the privilege.

EACH MARKET IS UNIQUE

If you were to design a studio specializing in children's portraits from the ground up, how would it look? What would the scale of the furniture and props be? What kind of music would you play? How would you light the reception area? I think you get my point. Now imagine you are designing a studio that only photographed high school seniors. Would it look different or would it be the same? The lighting, music, scale, would all have a different look and feel. So would a studio that specialized in just weddings, executive portraits, commercial photography, etc. Each type of photography serves a unique market. If you have a studio that offers more than one type of photography, you need to make compromises in your studio's design. If you were the buying public, which studio would you want to have your photography done by?

CONFUSED PROSPECTS DON'T BY (FROM YOU)

Most people can only process one message at a time. Have you ever been involved in a conversation where more than one person is speaking at the same time? It is confusing and distracting. It is a struggle just to follow one of the speakers and often you end up not following either one.

Offering a choice when a choice is not really necessary can only muddle the situation. When people are confused they are less likely to make a purchase decision. In a competitive marketplace, people won't take the time to decipher your marketing message, they simply move on to your competition.

In the early 1990's a local company called *Boston Chicken* invented a new category of fast food known as rotisserie chicken. The company offered only one product—you guessed it rotisserie chicken, plus side dishes (they had the best butternut squash I ever had). The company was a huge success. Several years ago the original owners decided to sell their chain of restaurants. The new owner immediately changed the name to *Boston Market*, added sandwiches, turkey, ham, and a host of other products to the menu and took the concept nationally. Not surprisingly, the restaurant has never been the same. They changed what made the company successful in the first place. (They even changed the recipe for my beloved butternut squash!) The restaurant lost its uniqueness and became just another place for fast food. The company has since closed many of its stores and was recently purchased by McDonald's.

In creating an ad or marketing campaign, think of what *single message* your prospect needs to hear in order to be *instantly interested and motivated* about your goods and services? The message should have a strong emotional pull that will make people want to change their plans to have you as their photographer.

PAST SUCCESS DOES NOT GUARANTEE FUTURE SUCCESS

One of the most successful animal species in the history of our planet was the dinosaur. These animals lived for over 160 million years! Yet today they are extinct. Past success is no guarantee of future viability. The newspapers are full of stories of companies that, after decades of success have closed their doors:

- TWA
- Montgomery Ward
- Smith-Corona
- Etc.

More often than not, the reason for the company's demise was a failure to adapt to a changing business environment. While they were once a big deal, they missed the warning signs that the market was changing and like the dinosaurs, many have disappeared, virtually overnight.

The big trend in retail over the past decade is mega-stores. Look at Home Depot, Staples, Barnes and Noble, Wal-Mart, Blockbuster Video, etc. These companies have huge stores, an almost endless inventory, and a large selection of items at "competitive" prices. If you try to compete with these giants on price or even selection, you are going to lose. Which is exactly what has happened to many of their competitors. Yet some companies have not only survived, they have thrived. Why? They adapted by either changing their niche or creating a new one.

The next step is to create a compelling message that will make your target audience see you out.

Unique Selling Proposition

Almost without exception, every book, or lecture I've heard on marketing and promoting your business mentions the need to create a niche. I've heard a niche described in many ways, but the best definition is the original, Unique Selling Proposition or (USP). The concept of having a USP was first coined by advertising great, Rosser Reeves in his 1960's book, *Reality in Advertising* (which is now out of print). Although created over 40 years ago, his original definition still rings true today:[14]

UNIQUE SELLING PROPOSITION DEFINED

1. Each ad must make a proposition to the consumer. Not just words, not just product puffery, not just show—window advertising. Each ad must say to each reader: "Buy this product, and you will get this specific benefit."

2. The proposition must be one that the competition either cannot, or does not offer. It must be unique— either a uniqueness of the brand or a claim not otherwise made in that particular field of advertising.

3. The proposition must be so strong that it can move the mass millions.

---

[14] *Differentiate Or Die—Survival In Our Era Of Killer Competition,* ©2000, Jack Trout with Steve Rivkin, John Wiley & Sons, Inc.

Become Indispensable To Your Clients

Your USP statement should create a strong emotional pull that makes your target audience want to use your services—so much so that they are willing to change their plans to ensure that you will be their photographer. Once created, your USP is the concept around which all of your marketing is based.

I like to illustrate the USP concept by giving two examples: one of a USP that didn't work and another that was very effective. Both are from my own experience.

The first USP example relates to wedding photography. I came up with, what I thought was a brilliant idea, of offering a money-back guarantee on my wedding photography services. Putting this USP to the test, it meets the first criteria, hire Till Photography, and you will get this specific benefit (money-back guarantee). It also met the second criteria; it was something no other studio in my area was offering. However, it did not pass the third test. My target audience did not find the benefit of value and thus the USP did not work.

However, I did develop a USP for business portraits that work very well. I realized that most people looking for a headshot were not interested in a work of art. They needed a clean photo of themselves for publicity purposes only. My USP: "I help business professionals to double or triple their marketing results by incorporating themselves into their collateral material." I developed an entire program, including a seminar and audiotape to support the USP. This time it was very successful because it passed all three criteria.

A USP Simplifies Your Message

What companies do you think of when you hear the following?

- Pizza delivered in 30 minutes or less
- Melts in your mouth, not in your hand
- The ultimate driving machine
- We try harder

Chances are your answers were, *Domino's Pizza, M&M Candy, BMW, and AVIS.* These companies have distinguished themselves from their competition by capitalizing on the three facets of a successful USP:

- Purchase our product you will receive a specific benefit,
- The benefit is one no-one else can offer, and
- Their target audience seeks *them* out

Each USP contains what I call *A Statement of Indispensability™*

STATEMENT OF INDISPENSABILITY™

A statement with strong emotional pull that makes people want to use your services—so much so that people are willing to change their plans to ensure that you will be their photographer. Once created, it is the concept around which all of your marketing is based.

Become Indispensable To Your Clients

Take a few moments and take a stab at creating your own USP. It doesn't have to be perfect, at least not yet. But the process will make you think of where you are today and where you want to go.

WORK FROM A POSITION OF STRENGTH

Everyone has strengths and weaknesses. While I am all for self-improvement, in terms of creating a lucrative niche, you are far better off to accentuate your strengths and don't worry about your weaknesses.

Audit your strengths from your client's viewpoint and rank them in order of importance. Implement a niche that plays to your strengths and against your competitors' weaknesses.

COMPETITIVE ASSESSMENT WORKSHEET

1. *Competitive uniqueness*—Do you offer any product, service, technology that is only available at your studio?)

   _____

2. *Competitive advantage*—You and your competitors offer the same service, but yours is better—such as speed of delivery or quality of work.)_____

   _____

3. *Competitive parity*—Both you and your competition offers or uses the exact same product/service, such as film, labs, albums, equipment, etc.)_____

   _____

4. *Competitive disadvantage*—Areas where your competition is better than you.) _____

   _____

The Lucrative Photographer

Select A Niche That You Can Dominate

In every market there are usually one or two dominant players, who have control over a significant share of the market (remember brand names). The mistake many business owners make is that they try to topple the giant. With few exceptions, the time, money, and resources it would take to do so are prohibitive. Market leaders are well entrenched, and for the most part, the public is reluctant to change. Yet each market leader has an Achilles heel, a weakness that can be exploited. These are the battles worth fighting.

For example, in your community there may be one or several studios that dominate the high school senior market. To try to beat these studios at their own game is foolish. They have the name, experience, and financial clout to ward off most challengers. Instead offer seniors something the big boys can't. Maybe all of your work is done on location, or only in black and white. Your goal, in this instance, is not to be the number one photographer to all high school seniors, just the photographer for those students who want a more personalized portrait or something unique.

By occupying a small section (niche) of the market you are not a threat to the big studios. Before long, you will have a reputation for your unique style and then you are the dominant player in your niche. Far fetched?

This is exactly what the Boston Beer Company, brewers of Sam Adams beer did. Their first ads used to make fun of the fact that the big companies spilled more beer each year than they brewed. Micro-brewed beers represent a niche product. Even today they represent a very small portion of the market. By the time the big beer makers took notice, the Boston Beer Company held a dominant position in their niche. Remember: choose your battles wisely.

SEEK A SERVICE NICHE

It is easier to distinguish yourself from a service aspect than from a product aspect. The simple fact is that much of what we photograph is very similar to what our competitors do. After all, we see each other's work in magazines and print competitions and if we like it, we copy it. Very little is truly unique. Customer service on the other hand is much harder to copy. To begin with, good customer service is rare, and exceptional service is almost non-existent. How often do you get a call after you purchase a product or use a service from a company thanking you for your patronage and asking if everything is satisfactory?

Even if your competitors copy your customer service procedures, they will NEVER implement them exactly the way you do. If the competition were concerned about customer service in the first place, it wouldn't be the rare commodity it is today.

The good news is that great customer service costs no more than average service (less if you consider the problems it can prevent and the new business it can generate). Find out what your ideal client would like to see changed in how photographers do business and change it.

The Lucrative Photographer

SEEK A LUCRATIVE NICHE

The most important thing you need as a business owner is an abundance of lucrative customers. It is one thing to find a customer who is willing to invest $3-4,000 per family portrait. It is entirely different to find enough of those customers to support your business on an ongoing basis. Make sure you ask yourself whether the niche you have chosen is large enough to cover your present and future needs.

PRE-EXISTING CONDITIONS

Who you do business with today will directly impact with whom you'll do business tomorrow. This is why it is essential that you clearly know who your target audience is, and who it is not.

If you could create the ideal client, what would he or she be like? What do they do for a living? Do they have children? Are they retired? All too often, photographers use income as the primary criterion in choosing whom they would like to market to.

While income may be an important aspect of your target audience, it may not be the only qualification. People need to value what you do in order to invest the amount of money you would like.

A good place to start is to ask, "What work or life conditions must *pre-exist* for each of your products/services *before* a prospect becomes a prime candidate for your services?" For example: Engaged to be married, a senior in high school, expecting parent, etc.)

51

Become Indispensable To Your Clients

Using the worksheet below, identify all pre-existing life/work conditions for each product or service you offer.

PRE-EXISTING LIFE/WORK CONDITIONS:

Product/Service: _____

_____

_____

_____

_____

While pre-existing life and/or work conditions make it easier to identify prospects that have a need for the products or services you offer, the same is true for your competition. This is one of the reasons why there are so many wedding and high school senior photographers.

Create A Positive Experience

Have you ever gone into a store and just couldn't wait to leave? Maybe it was the music, or the lighting, or maybe it was the salesperson, whatever the reason, your experience, was such that you'll most likely never visit the store again. On the other hand, when we've enjoyed the experience we don't want to leave. You feel at home, or at least very comfortable. Most likely you spent a lot more than you expected to, but it didn't matter—it was a great experience.

Notice that I did not mention the quality of the product or service. Both stores could have offered identical products; however, it was the experience that you remembered. I'm sure many of you have had the occasion to photograph someone's wedding, social event, or family portrait where their brother, sister, or friend had used another photographer. Like me, you probably asked why they didn't choose the same photographer themselves. Sometimes the other photographer was booked or had retired, and for some they simply didn't like the quality of the photography. However, more often than not, it has been my experience that the client was making a change because they didn't have a positive experience. It is interesting to note that photographers rated their personality as the second most important reason why their clients hired them. Ironically it may also be the reason why some people don't return.

Earlier I said that it is easier to create a niche around customer service than it is to create a niche around a product or service. Why? Because the number one reason people change from one company to another is due to a feeling of indifference (67%). In short, they feel neglected, leaving them with a less than satisfying experience.

This is not to say that quality doesn't matter, because it does, but only to a point. Throughout this book I am assuming you can produce professional quality images that are more than adequate for your clientele. Having a great experience is not a substitute for quality photography. However, customer service can distinguish you from your competition and make people seek you out.

ENGAGE YOUR CLIENTS

B. Joseph Pine II and James Gilmore in their book, *The Experience Economy* suggests that companies should create an experience that people would otherwise pay to have. They believe that if you were to charge admission just to visit your studio, you would need to create an experience and environment that offers a lot more than simply showing frames, albums, and prints. What is lacking is an experience that will *engage* your clients.

One of the best examples of a company that engages their clientele is a local company named Jordan's Furniture. In one of their stores they have a Motion Odyssey Movie (MOM) where the seats move so you feel like you're moving but you're not. In another store they re-created Bourbon Street, New Orleans, complete with a Dixieland band, free beads, and a FX Mardi Gras Show. Are their stores lucrative? The average retail furniture store in the U.S. grosses about $150 per square foot, per month. Jordan's is close to $1,000 per square foot per month—nine times the national average. Is the furniture at Jordan's better than furniture at other stores? No, they carry the same brands as lots of other stores. Their prices are not lower either, and in some cases they're higher. They also *never have a sale*. So how do they do it? They sell furniture as entertainment. They have created an experience that people want to repeat over and over again. People bring their friends and relatives who visit from out of town to the stores to show them what it is all about. Can you say the same thing about your studio?

Another company that does an excellent job in engaging their clients is Illuminations, a candle and gift specialty store. In my area, the store is located in a large mall. As anyone who has been in a mall can attest to, they are brightly lit and somewhat noisy. When you enter Illuminations, it is a completely different experience. The lighting is soft and subtle (to show off the candles) and the music is soft and soothing. They have made it easy and enjoyable to spend time, shop, and of course, buy—which we frequently do.

Engaging your clients increases your product's perceived value. You are no longer simply offering a product; instead you are providing a valuable service. The greater the perceived value, the more a person is willing to pay for your service.

Let's assume for a moment that you photograph children—what if you had a play area for them complete with all sorts of toys? How about having a weekly storytelling hour or costume party? Maybe you could do something special on each child's birthday? By engaging your clients you create an environment your target audience covets, independent of your primary service. The benefit to you is the more often they visit your studio, the more likely they are to use your services and tell their friends. Pine and Gilmore are careful to point out that these services don't necessarily have to be free of charge, although you may want to consider providing these added benefits as a perk for your very best clients.

FEDEX AND DISNEY

I once read that today's clients expect products and services to be delivered with the speed of FedEx and with the style and quality of Disney. It's easy to understand why. In today's economic environment, people want everything yesterday. People can log onto the Internet or pick up the phone and order merchandise 24 hours a day. For many people, regular UPS is not good enough; people are often willing to pay extra to have their purchase shipped to them the next day. With respect to software, you can download the product immediately. The public's patience with delivery shrinks every day. Disney is the benchmark against which all customer service and experience are measured. Both of these companies have raised the bar with respect to customer service. How does your studio measure up?

Capitalizing on this shift in client expectations is vital to the long-term survival of any company. If your normal turnaround time for a portrait is 4-6 weeks and

The Lucrative Photographer

a competitor, who *offers a similar quality product,* can produce it in 24 hours, which studio do you think the public will choose? Think about how important delivery time is to you with your vendors. I know lots of photographers who have changed labs or album manufacturers because of lengthy delays in turnaround.

Create A Professional Image

Creating a WOW experience includes having a professional image. For most clients, their first experience with you and your studio is over the phone. Going back to my days as a financial planner, I am convinced people can hear you "smile" on the phone. You can always tell when someone is in a bad mood or isn't really paying attention. When you speak to someone like this, how do you feel—not very important? You are always better off letting your voice mail answer the phone if you can't answer your phone with a smile. Which leads me to my next point—voice mail.

In today's environment, there is no excuse for not having a voice mail system. Most phone companies offer the service at a nominal cost. Voice mail sounds infinitely superior to the traditional answering machine. People have answering machines; professional businesses have voice mail. When I call a company that has an answering machine it says to me that they are either just starting out, or they're cheap; either way they are starting with one strike against them.

One of the best messages I have ever heard is from Brian and Judith Shindle, of *Creative Moments Photography*, in Westerville, Ohio. The message provided the usual information but it was presented in a very warm and romantic way. I wanted to hire them based on the quality of the message alone.

The Lucrative Photographer

Remember that competition for your services is strong. In an area where there is more than one quality photographer, it is the little things that will distinguish you from everyone else. Don't give a prospect a reason NOT to hire you.

PEOPLE SEE WITH THEIR EARS AND HEAR WITH THEIR EYES

You passed the phone test and you have an appointment to meet your prospective client. What does the following say about you and your company?

PROFESSIONAL IMAGE TEST

- What do people see when they walk into your studio?
- Does the environment match the image you're trying to create?
- If your studio is in your home, is it separate from your living space?
- What type of lighting do you have?
- What type of music is playing in the background?
- How do you present yourself when you greet and work with clients?
- Is your collateral material professional? (Price lists, brochures, business card, logo, etc).

When I photograph weddings I always wear a tuxedo. Not because every event is black-tie, but clients want to know that I will be dressed appropriately. People wouldn't ask the question, if they or someone they know didn't have a problem with another photographer. If you want to be treated as a professional, you need to act and dress like one to begin with.

One of the finest studios I have ever visited is *Derby Studios* in Salem, Massachusetts. The owners, Michael and Louise Skerry, are two of the most sought after wedding photographers in the Boston area. Michael and Louise understand the importance of making a great first impression. Prior to decorating their studio, they did their homework. The colors on the walls and the lighting were chosen to accentuate their photographs. They have an arrangement with a florist to provide fresh flowers every week. There is always soft music playing in the background and clients are provided with a soft beverage in "distinctive" glasses and mugs. When you enter their studio, everything says luxury, quality, and professional.

Louise told me she read that you should spend twice as much as you think you should spend on the lobby to create a "wow" impression when people enter the studio. Successful retailers would agree. As a wedding photographer, I know from personal experience that the most elaborate decorations at any hotel are in their lobbies. Even in the most expensive of hotels, the actual rooms themselves are often quite plain compared to the lobby. I am not advocating going into debt just to redecorate your lobby or greeting area. Rather, I want to stress the importance of creating a strong first impression. If you are promoting yourself as a "high-end" photographer, your studio image needs to be on par with your work and your clients' expectations.

The Lucrative Photographer

There is nothing unprofessional about having a studio or office located in your home. Most photographers work out of their homes. However, it is vitally important that it looks professional and, if at all possible, be separate from your living space.

For many of you reading this book, I am sure your studio is appropriately decorated. If not, how can you expect your clients to take you seriously, if your studio does not look professional. How much faith would you have with your accountant, attorney, or doctor, if their offices looked similar to yours?

Being a professional is not about working full-time or part-time, working out of your home, or in a retail location, nor is it about wearing a tuxedo. It is about having reverence for yourself and your profession. Look at your studio and your image from the public's perspective. How much would you pay for you based on what you see? Look at where your (ideal) clients shop and give them an experience that is *at least* as impressive.

PRESENTATION IS EVERYTHING

A friend of mine once gave me a Mont Blanc pen as a gift. What impressed me (besides the gesture itself) was the packaging of the pen. The presentation is wonderful. It comes in a well-padded custom-fitted case, which includes a 20-page instruction manual, for a pen!

In case you're wondering, Mont Blanc pens retail for over $165. That is a lot of Bics. You don't have to be a pen aficionado to be impressed with a Mont Blanc. Their packaging says it all, "The Art of Writing". They have positioned themselves as a pen people aspire to own (and gift). When you purchase a Mont Blanc, you don't ask how much, it is simply a matter of color and style.

The Mont Blanc example is not unique. Smart business professionals know that presentation can enhance or detract from a product's perceived value. Why are people willing to spend two to five times for a meal at a "fine dining" restaurant when they can get a similar product at a family style restaurant? Why do people spend hundreds (and even thousands) of dollars for a watch when a Timex™ can keep time just as well?

Each of the examples above illustrate that people are willing to pay a premium for a product or service even though lower priced alternatives exist (sound familiar?) The key is *perceived* value. In the case of the Mont Blanc pen or watch, it is the prestige associated with owning the product. With the restaurant, it is the ambiance and the service associated with the fine dining experience. Would these products and services have the same prestige if they were presented in a generic/ordinary way? These products and services command a premium price in part because of the way they are packaged and presented.

This is a good lesson for photographers to heed. How we present our products (and ourselves) says a lot about how our clients will perceive its worth. How do you deliver your finished prints, albums, and wall portraits? Are the prints delivered loose or in the glassine bags from the lab? Does the way you present your images to your clients increase or decrease their perceived value?

Many of us (myself included) have been guilty of poor product presentation from time to time. This is especially true for photographers just starting their business. As the quality of your work (and your prices) increase, so does the need for you to improve your product presentation.

Presentation does not begin with the delivery of the product; it starts with the studio's décor, your dress, and how you greet people. Companies that offer premium products and services have premium facilities. When you go out for fine dining, you expect the ambiance to be superior to that found at a family style restaurant. The same is true of your studio. What does your studio's décor say about the quality of your work?

How you handle the photographs is also important. We use white cotton gloves to show our work to clients and prospects. It sends a subtle message that the photographs are valuable and should be handled with care. As an aside, when a bride and groom view their images, we have them wear the gloves as well. Invariably one of them (usually the groom) will take off the gloves and touch a print. The bride will always reprimand him to put the gloves back on. She doesn't want him to damage her photographs. We have just elevated the product (and our sale) from pictures to a treasured possession.

Become Indispensable To Your Clients

The same is true for how you deliver your product. I am embarrassed to say that we use to deliver the prints in the same bags the lab use to deliver the prints to us. Shame on me! We have since gone to delivering prints in presentation boxes embossed with our studio name. The prints are wrapped in tissue and the box has a ribbon on the outside. Whenever possible, we want our clients to pick up their albums in our studio, rather than shipping the album to them. We want the presentation of the finished album to be a big deal.

If we don't take pride in our work, why should the public? Look at the way you present yourself and your photography to the public. Does your presentation enhance or detract from the image you are trying to convey? If your presentation is not increasing your products perceived value, look for ways to change. The quality of our photography is important, but how much the public will pay can be greatly influenced by how it is presented to them.

Summary

As important as having a specialty is, it does not preclude you offering secondary services. When I explain the importance of having a narrowly defined niche to photographers, I often get the response yes, but....

Being a photographic specialist runs contrary to conventional studio wisdom, which is the "cradle to grave" mentality. That is, you photograph someone's high school senior portrait, which leads to a portrait of the whole family, then a wedding, his or her kids, etc.

In the end you become just another studio that does a little of this and a little of that.

RESOURCES

BOOKS

Selling The Invisible: A Field Guide To Modern Marketing, Harry Beckwith, ©1997, Warner Books.

Price Wars: How To Win The Battle For Your Customer!, Thomas J. Winninger, ©1994, St. Thomas Press.

FOCUS: The Future Of Your Company Depends On It, Al Ries, ©1997, Harper Business.

The Twenty-Two Immutable Laws of Branding, Al Ries and Laura Ries, ©1998 Harper Business

The Experience Economy: Work Is Theatre & Every Business A Stage, ©1999, B. Joseph Pine, II and James H. Gilmore, Harvard Business School Press.

Selling The Invisible: A Field Guide To Modern Marketing, Harry Beckwith, ©1997, Warner Books.

AUDIO TAPES

Personal Performance, Empowering Your Life and Your Career, ©1995, Thomas J. Winninger, CSP, CPAE, Winninger Resource Group, (612) 896-1900

Become Indispensable To Your Clients

CONSULTANTS
JMB Marketing, Bob Martel, 210 Clover Hill Street, Marlborough, Massachusetts 01752-6013, (508) 481-8383, www.info@jmbmarketing.com

21ˢᵗ Century Management Consulting, Inc., 25 Grant St, Suite 1, Waltham, Massachusetts 02453-4201, (781) 899-4210. www.21stCenturyMgmt.com.

Maximize Your Profitability

☞ Are You Really Profitable?

☞ How Do You Know How Much To Charge, If You Don't Know How Much It Costs?

☞ The Seven Deadly "Credit" Sins

☞ Endless Cash

☞ Are You Ready For Prime Time?

☞ Lucrative Pricing Strategies

Are You Really Profitable?

If I asked you whether or not your studio made a profit last year, the odds are your response would be yes. And why not, your profit and loss statement says you made money, and you're showing a profit on your taxes. But are you really lucrative? It is this very question that in part motivated me to become a consultant and write this book. As I lecture around the country, I am constantly amazed at how many photographers believe they are profitable, when in fact they are actually losing money.

How is this possible you ask? To answer this apparent paradox, let's look at an example: Suppose your studio had annual sales of $125,000 and paid cash expenses of $85,000. How many of you think your salary/studio profit is $40,000? If you're like most photographers, you probably answered yes. Why? Because many photographers work on the assumption that salary equals studio profit and therefore fluctuates, depending on how good a year you're having.

SIMPLE STUDIO PROFIT/LOSS STATEMENT	
Annual Studio Sales	$125,000[15]
Cost of Goods Sold	($38,500[16])
Paid Fixed Expenses	($46,500)
Salary/Profit?	$40,000

---

[15] Based on Median Gross Sales from Census 2000
[16] Census 2000 (31% of sales)

The Lucrative Photographer

It is easy to understand the basis of one's confusion. As noted in the survey, 75% of all photographers operate as sole proprietors. As a sole proprietor, salary and studio profit are one in the same on your tax return. Since the IRS does not distinguish salary from studio profit, most photographers do not either. If neither your accountant nor the IRS asks you to separate salary from studio profit can it really be that important? As we'll see shortly, the distinction can be the difference between profit and loss.

SALARY IS A FIXED, NOT VARIABLE, EXPENSE

Let's begin with how we treat the owner's salary. How many of you would reply to a job want ad that would require you to work both day and evening, six sometimes seven days a week, including holidays, *without knowing if or how much money you would be paid?*

Yet isn't that exactly what many photographers do? If I asked you to tell me what your annual income will be at the beginning of the year, would you be able to do so? How many of you don't know how much you earned until after your accountant tells you? How long would you expect your employees to stay with you, if you paid them the way you pay yourself?

When I asked photographers to tell me how they paid themselves, only 27% responded by saying they paid themselves a fixed salary on a fixed and/or regular basis. The others paid themselves as funds allowed or when they needed the money. *An owner's salary should be based on your individual economic needs and photographic experience, not your sales volume.* To operate a business any other way would make paying your personal financial obligations, such as your rent or mortgage, very difficult—which sadly is the case for many in our profession.

Paying yourself a fixed salary has an added benefit of forcing you to meet a payroll (even if you are the only employee). It is an indicator of how well your business is doing. If you can't make payroll on a consistent basis, you don't have a profitable business. On the other hand, if you are having an exceptional year, you can pay yourself a bonus at year's end or reinvest the money back into the business.

> *Note: When you're new in business your salary may not be what it needs to be. This is why, before you begin a business venture, it is important for you to have plenty of cash in reserve. This allows you to pay your personal bills while you grow your business to a level that can sustain you and your family.*

The exact amount of salary you pay yourself is a personal decision. It is better to start off with a modest salary and pay yourself a bonus, than to withdraw too much money and run out of cash when you need it the most. No matter what your salary is, it is a fixed, not a variable, expense.

Let's go back to our example. By including a salary of $25,000, our studio's profit drops from $40,000 to $15,000. So far so good, but we're not done yet.

STUDIO PROFIT/LOSS AFTER ADJUSTING FOR OWNER'S SALARY

Annual studio sales	$125,000
COGS	($38,500)
Fixed Expenses	($46,500)
Owner's salary	($25,000)[17]
Adjusted profit?	$15,000

NON-CASH EXPENSES

The next adjustment to our studio's profit and loss statement (P&L) is your studio's non-cash expenses. Non-cash expenses are expenditures your business incurs without the need to actually write out a check. Three of the most common non-cash expenses photographers are likely to encounter are depreciation, mileage, and use of one's home.

Depreciation is one of the more complex accounting matters many small businesses face. Probably because most photographers don't understand how it works or the impact it has on their bottom line. For many of us, our annual equipment purchases are fairly modest. Each year we make our equipment purchases and deduct the entire amount of the purchase on our current year's taxes. However, in today's digital age, it is possible for a studio to spend $25,000 or more in a single year on new equipment. When your annual equipment purchases exceed a certain dollar amount

---

[17] Estimate based on the average salary reported in the Census 2000

($24,000 for 2002 and $25,000 for 2003) you are required to spread out, or *amortize*, the cost of the equipment over a period of time. The number of years is based on what the IRS determines to be the equipment's "useful life." For example, let's assume you purchase $30,000 on new equipment this year. In 2002, you will be permitted to expense (deduct the amount on the 2002 tax return) $24,000 of the $30,000 you purchased, even though you paid for the equipment in its entirety this year. The remaining $6,000 is deducted from your taxes over a period of years based on a schedule determined by the IRS.

Most accounting software allows for depreciation, and your accountant can assist you with the amount of the deduction you are permitted each year, if applicable. For our purposes, it is important to note that in subsequent years you will account for an expense against which no cash will be spent. (As we'll see later in the section on cash management, non-cash expenses can have a dramatic impact on our ability to make future investments in equipment.)

Another common non-cash expense is mileage. If you travel to and from a photographic assignment, you might be eligible for a mileage deduction on your taxes.[18] If so, the deduction is most likely a non-cash expense. You don't need to write a check each month to receive the tax deduction at year-end. However,

---

[18] Note: Each person's business structure and situation varies, these examples are not intended to be tax advice, but rather an example of a possible deduction. Please consult your accountant for any tax-related matters.

unlike depreciation, most accounting software packages do not track non-cash of expenses, therefore, it must be done manually. Fortunately, there are easy solutions to help you track non-cash expenses and give you a true reflection of your studio's profitability. The easiest and simplest solution is to use a spreadsheet to list non-cash expenses. Once you set up the spreadsheet it should take you no more than 10-15 minutes per month to make the necessary adjustments. (Note: QuickBooks Pro will automatically transfer your Profit and Loss statement to an Excel spreadsheet).

Our last example is deducting the use of your home as an office. If you operate your business out of your home, you may be eligible for a deduction on your taxes for the portion your of your home specifically devoted to your business. As with mileage, you receive a tax benefit, but you most likely do not pay yourself rent. The IRS has strict guidelines on how much of a deduction you can take on your taxes. However, it is a good idea to take into account how much it would cost to have an office/studio outside your home in preparing your prices. Remember, our objective is to get a true reflection of your business' financial health.

Returning to our original example, a studio's true profitability depends on whether you take into account ALL of the expenses (cash and non-cash) associated with running the business. To determine your studio's true profit or loss, we need to adjust the operating income/loss to reflect any non-cash expenses you may have incurred.

Our original gross profit of $40,000 has quickly dropped to $10,000. We're still in the black, but we're also not finished.

STUDIO PROFIT/LOSS AFTER
ADJUSTING FOR NON-CASH EXPENSES

Annual studio sales	$125,000
COGS	($38,500)
Fixed Expenses	($46,500)
Owner's salary	($25,000)
Depreciation (prior year purchases)	($5,000)[19]
Adjusted profit?	$10,000

EXPENSES THAT DON'T APPEAR ON YOUR TAXES

Don't look for this in an accounting textbook or even from your accountant. Technically, there's no such thing. Now before you get that confused look on your face and go back to see if you read the last sentence correctly, let me explain. *Non-tax expenses* are expenses that your business may not need to pay, but a typical conventional business would normally incur. For example: medical insurance and related employee benefits.

Many photographers (including me) receive their medical insurance from their spouse, while others receive coverage from their regular full-time job. In this example, photographers are receiving an employee benefit but not actually paying for it (at least the business is not). To get a true reflection of your

---

[19] Census 2000, depreciation is 4% of sales

company's profitability, you should take into account what this benefit would cost you, if your business actually paid for it.

Some of you might think this is just a matter of semantics, after-all why do you need to keep track of something you don't pay for and can't deduct on your taxes? The answer is simple, someday you might need to pay these expenses, and if you don't take them into account, you may not be able to pay for them if you need to. If your spouse loses his or her job, where would the medical insurance coverage come from? Maybe you want to make the transition from part-time to full-time. Unless you take these expenses into account, you may never generate enough sales revenue to make the transition. Finally, you're simply undervaluing your work. If you're serious about owning a business, you must act accordingly. By taking all these "expenses" into account, it forces you to charge real money for your services. As we've seen earlier, prices that make us sound like a bargain can actually make us look second rate. To be respected as professionals it is important that we act and charge for our services accordingly.

As you can see below, our original $40,000 profit has become a break-even proposition. In this instance the non-taxable expenses represent employee benefits. Using a common rule of thumb, which says employee benefits are generally 40% of salary, resulted in the $10,000.[20] While some of you may disagree with the

---

[20] According the US Chamber of Commerce, employee benefits as a percentage of salary ranges from 38% to 45% or higher.

numbers I've used, the concept behind the numbers is financially sound. In this example, the loss is a paper loss, since the cost of the employee benefits was not actually paid for by the studio. However, it does illustrate that many photographers operate under the belief that they are making money when in fact they are really losing money. By not taking into account all of the expenses a business traditionally incurs, you undervalue your work. This is the difference between treating your profession as a hobby versus treating it as a business.

I urge you to revisit your P&L as soon as you can. Make the adjustments I've shown here, and determine whether you are indeed making a profit or are incurring a loss. Even if you are in the red, all is not lost, as you'll soon see.

STUDIO PROFIT/LOSS AFTER ADJUSTING FOR NON-TAXABLE EXPENSES

Annual studio sales	$125,000
COGS	($38,500)
Fixed Expenses	($46,500)
Owner's salary	($25,000)
Depreciation (prior year purchases)	($5,000)
Employee Benefits rec'd not paid	($10,000)
Net income (loss)	$0

How Do You Know How Much To Charge, If You Don't Know How Much It Costs?

MINIMUM SALARY REQUIREMENTS

The first step in developing a lucrative pricing structure is to know what your *minimum salary* should be. Your salary should be based not only on what you need to pay your bills, it should also include compensation for the additional risks associated with owning your own business. In 1999 our neighbor's son graduated from Boston College with a degree in finance. His *starting* salary was over $50,000. If you were to add in employee benefits, his total compensation is almost $70,000![21] How many photographers do you know earn a salary in excess of $70,000 from just their photography? Don't forget he gets paid vacations, paid holidays, and weekends off. Plus he doesn't have the stress and responsibility of owning his own company.

Depending on what part of the country you're from, your minimum salary requirements will vary. However, I have asked photographers around the country what they think their minimum salary should be, and most people responded that they would like to have a salary between $40-$50,000. Unfortunately, as we've seen in my survey, the average photographer makes significantly less.

---

[21] According the US Chamber of Commerce, employee benefits as a percentage of salary ranges from 38% to 45% or higher.

Maximize Your Profitability

In order to determine your minimum salary requirements, you should first do a personal expense budget. As with any budget, list all the categories for which you will spend money. You should include only personal expenses in this budget. (Programs like Microsoft Money and Quicken can help with the budgetary process.) Don't forget to budget money for vacation and fun. Remember, your personal budget is paid from *after-tax* income. To determine your minimum salary requirements, you will need to make an adjustment for taxes. That is, how much do you need to take home in order to have enough money to pay your bills after you have paid your taxes?

MINIMUM SALARY REQUIREMENT ILLUSTRATION

Total personal expenses	$40,000
Total tax rate (estimate)	28%
Gross Income needed to pay expenses*	$55,555

*Formula (Income/(1-tax rate) or $30,000/(1-.28)

In the example above, if you need to have $40,000 of net, after-tax income and your total tax rate is 28% you will need to earn a salary of $55,555. This is the figure you would use as your salary in determining your break-even sales point for your business, as you'll soon see.

THE DREADED "B" WORD

Now that you have determined your base salary, you need to establish a budget for your business. I think people shy away from creating a budget because first of all it's not fun and second, people don't know where to begin. As we've seen above, your budget should include not only your cash (out of pocket expenses) but also non-cash and non-tax expenses as well.

Zero-Based Budgeting

A common mistake people make in creating a budget is simply taking what they paid in expenses last year and either use the exact same figure for the current year or they will add 4-5% to cover inflation. On the surface this makes perfect sense. But there is a flaw in the logic. It assumes that everything else has remained the same—that you will be photographing the same number of sessions, using the same marketing programs, the same photographic techniques, etc.

In any given year it is easy begin to stray from your intended niche. If you simply roll-forward your budget from year to year, you would not make any course corrections, if need be. Before you know it you're way off course and again adrift without a niche. With zero-based budgeting you start each year from scratch as if it was your first year in business. Each year you need to re-evaluate your current business situation, make necessary adjustments based on the current economic climate and what direction you would like to take your business, and plan for the upcoming year accordingly.

If you need to borrow money, your bank will also want not only a budget for the current year, but also for the subsequent two years as well. In this instance, it is ok to project or "roll forward" what you expect your future budget to look like based on your current situation. This is known as a *three-year rolling budget*.

But for our purposes let's focus on creating a budget for the current year.

FIXED VERSUS VARIABLE EXPENSES

For any business there are only two types of expenses: fixed and variable. Fixed expenses are those that must be paid regardless of whether you had any sales or not, for example—rent, salary, loans, utilities, etc. Fixed expenses can be broken down into six general categories: Salary and Benefits; Administration; Marketing; Auto; Building Overhead; and Equipment Purchases. In addition, we must also include our non-cash expenses such as Depreciation, Mileage, and Use of Home.

By comparison, variable expenses are directly related to sales. Without sales, there would be no expense. Examples of variable expenses include lab expense, film, albums, photographic assistants, etc. With few exceptions, all variable expenses associated with running a photography studio can be categorized as Cost of Goods Sold (CGS).

BREAK-EVEN AND THE BUDGETARY PROCESS

Over the years I have tried a lot of different ways to explain how to put together a budget and calculate the break-even sales amount. By far the way that has worked best was to create a studio from scratch and actually go through the budgetary process using figures created by real photographers. For simplicity purposes, in the example below, I have assumed there is just one photographer and no other employees. Furthermore, the only services offered will be weddings, portraits, and high school seniors. (A detailed listing of all the expense categories can be found in the appendix.)

In the following example, our studio is located in a rural (New England) location. Note the *budgetary figures were provided by photographers as being a fair representation of the expenses in their area.* (In preparing your budget, you will be using your own figures.) As always, we start with the owner's salary. Our owner's salary, as noted above is $55,555. Added to the base salary is the cost of employee benefits, such as medical insurance (life, health, disability, vacation, retirement, etc.), which in most companies is assumed to be approximately 40% of salary, in our example $22,222. Total owner's salary including employee benefits is $77,777.

The next category is *marketing*, which generally runs 5-10% of sales. Marketing includes print ads, web page design and hosting, brochures, yellow pages, client appreciation, networking, etc. In our example we have assumed a marketing expense of $10,000.

Administration is the day-to-day expenses of operating your studio. In this category are bank fees (including the cost of offering credit cards), loan payments, education (attending seminars, conventions, etc.), membership and subscriptions, office supplies, professional services, etc.) In our example administration expense is $9,000.

ABC STUDIO BUDGET/BREAK-EVEN ANALYSIS

Fixed Expenses

Owner's salary	$55,555
Employee benefits (40% of salary)[22]	$22,222
Total employee benefits	*77,777*
Marketing	$10,000
Administration	$9,000
Auto (including auto Insurance)	$5,000
Building overhead (rent, mtg., or use of home)	$12,000
Equipment purchases	$12,000
Depreciation (prior year purchases)	$5,000
Total Fixed Expenses	$130,777
Gross Profit Margin (Sales – COGS)/Sales	$0.69[23]

Break-even = Fixed Expenses/Gross Profit Margin

Break-even: $130,777/(0.69)	$189,532
Studio profit* (10% of sales)	$18,953
Target sales level	$208,485

Sales mix (as a percent of sales)	
Weddings	40%
Portraits	40%
High School Seniors	20%

Sales mix (total number of sessions)	
Weddings	25
Portraits	80
High School Seniors	50

Minimum (break-even) sales, excluding profit per category	
Weddings	$3,033
Portraits	$948
High School Seniors	$758

*   Remember, our goal, as a business owner is not to break-even, but to make a fair profit (return on our investment) as well. You should consider studio profit in determining your prices.

---

[22] According the US Chamber of Commerce, employee benefits as a percentage of salary ranges from 38% to 45% or higher.
[23] Census 2000, COGS is 31% of sales

Next is *Automobile expense*. I prefer to separate out Auto expense from the administration because I deduct mileage as a non-cash expense. I find it easier to keep track of the expense this way. However, many people will include this under the administration category. Here I assume you are not leasing but in fact are taking a deduction for mileage. I have also included the insurance for your car. Total mileage expense for the year is expected to be $5,000. You may also want to include the cost of replacing your current car. That is, putting money aside each month for the necessary down payment for the purchase of your next vehicle (see section on cash management).

Building Overhead includes the use of your home, rent/mortgage, building maintenance, etc. If you work out of your home, you should at least include the tax benefit of doing so. In our example, I have assumed a 1,000 square foot studio at $10 per square foot plus $2,000 for maintenance for a total of $12,000 per year.

Next comes *Equipment Purchases*. This category includes all purchases for items such as lenses, computers, desks, etc. In today's environment, I expect most of us will be investing heavily in upgrading our digital capacities. Accordingly, our budget is $12,000 for the coming year.

Our final fixed expense is *Depreciation*. You should contact your accountant to calculate the amount (if any) you need to budget for this year's Depreciation. In our example, I have included a depreciation expense of $5,000 from purchases made in previous years based on data provided from the Census 2000.[24]

Our total fixed expense budget for the year is $130,777. We also need to budget for our variable expenses (Cost of Goods Sold). Since these expenses are directly related to sales, they are usually expressed as a percentage of sales. What is an appropriate percentage? Most lucrative studios have CGS of between 20-35% of sales. I have assumed a figure of 31% of sales based on the results from the Census 2000.

MINIMUM SALES REQUIREMENT

Break-even is the minimum amount of sales you need to generate in order to pay your salary and ALL of your business expenses. You can always go above break-even, but you should never go below. The formula is very simple:

> Break-even = Fixed Expenses/Gross Profit Margin

Gross Profit is total sales minus your cost of goods sold (those expenses that are directly related to producing your product). Gross Profit Margin (GPM) is Gross Profit expressed as a percentage of sales.

In other words, you will need to generate a minimum of $156,000 to pay all your bills.

---

[24] As with any tax matters, please consult your tax advisor.

BREAK-EVEN

Fixed Expenses = $130,777
Gross Profit Margin (GPM) = 69% of sales

Apply Formula
Break-even = $130,777/0.69 or $189,532

DON'T FORGET TO INCLUDE PROFIT!

Lucrative photographers are not in business to break-even; they're in business to make a profit. Think of your business as an investment. If your sales equal your principle, then profit is your return on your investment. In this instance I have assumed a 10% profit, which is what you could expect if you were investing your money. In our example, 10% equals $18,953 bringing our minimum sales requirement to $208,485.

PUTTING THE BUDGET INTO PRACTICE

Determining your minimum sales volume is only the first step. It doesn't tell you what you need to gross for each individual sitting. To do this we need to know what products and services you plan to offer. Our studio has decided that 40% of sales should come from both weddings and portraits. The remaining 20% will be from high school seniors.

If weddings represent 40% of our total sales volume, it is logical to assume it is also responsible for 40% of the expenses. (While this may not be entirely true, for our purposes it is close enough.) Consequently, the minimum sale for weddings would be $189,532 times

40% or $75,813. The same is true for portraits. Since high school seniors represents only 20% the total sales for this category is $37,906.

Now that we know what percentage of income each of the categories represents we need to determine how many sittings we plan to do. Our goal is to do 25 weddings, 80 family portraits, and 50 high school seniors. The last step is to determine what our break-even sales volume is on a per sitting basis. To calculate this amount we would divide $75,813 (total weddings sales) by 25 (the number of weddings we plan to photograph. Our minimum sale for weddings is $3,033. When we apply the same formula for portraits and high school seniors we get $948 and $758 respectively.

Now before you raise your hand and say, "My clients won't pay this for my services," this is just an example. To lower the minimum sales level you could increase the number of sittings you do or hire additional photographers. The point is you MUST go through this process in order to determine how much you NEED to charge. To a certain extent it doesn't matter what other photographers charge. You need to base your fees on what YOU need to earn. This is also why it is critically important that you have a well-defined niche. If you can provide a product or service that people desire and one that can be obtained only from your studio, you become indispensable to your clients and price becomes secondary. Keep in mind, photographers rank price as number five in order of importance in how clients choose them.

The Lucrative Photographer

Whenever I give this presentation to photographers, I sometimes feel I need to administer CPR to resuscitate some of the people in the audience. Unfortunately, as a whole, photographers have been grossly undervaluing their worth for quite sometime. If you find that after going through this process, your prices need to be raised dramatically, DON'T do it all at once. Create a plan that will bring your prices up to a profitable level over a 2-3 year period. Sure you will lose a few of your old clients, but the ones you replace them with will make you a lot more lucrative.

How important is your break-even sales level?

My research shows that studios that know their break-even levels, on average, gross 43% more than those who don't. In addition, these studios also earn 9% more in net income. In fact, next to having a written business plan, recognizing your studio's break-even sales figures is the most important factor in a studio's profitability.

Common Tax Planning Mistakes

I asked my tax advisor to offer tips on how to avoid the most common mistakes he sees clients make on their taxes. His top five (in no particular order) are as follows:

1. *Not taking full advantage of current year capital purchases*—As noted earlier, you can currently expense all equipment purchases up to $24,000. A common mistake business owners make is depreciating purchases over time they could have deducted in the year the purchase was made. A

good reason to work with a tax professional.

2. *Not properly deducting the business use of your car*—If you use your car for business you can either use the standard mileage deduction or your actual automotive expenses. The IRS does have specific rules and guidelines regarding switching from one method to the other. As with any deduction, the more complete your documentation is, the better.

3. *Not having a retirement plan*—As we'll discuss in the next chapter, very few photographers fully fund their retirement accounts each year. Besides being a sound investment in your future, retirement plans can provide significant tax benefits today.

4. *Not taking full advantage of the home-office deduction*—Many business owners are afraid to take the deduction because they believe it will create a red flag with the IRS. This is no longer the case and the tax laws have been relaxed to make it easier to benefit from the deduction.

5. *Not properly planning capital purchases*—If you were planning to make a large equipment purchase early next year and you had a large profit this year, it may be to your advantage to purchase the equipment prior to the current year's end so you will receive the full amount of the deduction in the current tax year.

The Lucrative Photographer

Taxes are a complex subject. However, with a little planning and proper advice you can go a long way towards maximizing the amount of money you get to keep.

The Seven Deadly "Credit" Sins

In the previous section, I talked about budgeting and accounting for equipment purchases. The assumption was made the equipment was purchased outright—you a paid for the equipment without the need of additional financing (borrowing money).

Paying cash (not borrowing money) for equipment is not always possible or desirable. There are times when borrowing money to make your purchase makes perfect economic sense.

If you have determined that borrowing money is appropriate, there are a few things you should be aware of. I contacted Bob Bell, president of *Independent Leasing Associates*, a full service lessor specializing in financing equipment for the imaging and graphic arts industry. Bob has earned the prestigious CLP designation, and is on the Board of Directors of the National Association of Equipment Leasing Brokers. I asked Bob to list some of the most common mistakes and errors business owners make when seeking financing for their equipment. Below is a list of Bob's "Seven Deadly Credit Sins"[25].

---

[25] As with any financial decision, please consult your accountant or business advisor before borrowing money.

SIN #1:
NOT HAVING TIME IN BUSINESS
FOR THE AMOUNT REQUESTED

It's how long you have owned this business, not how long the building has been there or how long the guy you bought it from was in business. If it is a retail operation how long have you owned it in this location? Just because you were successful in running a studio in Jacksonville, doesn't mean you will be successful in Miami. So the key is, "time in business under the current ownership at the present location". A lender might be comfortable loaning $50,000 to a two-year-old business but not $150,000. There are three key tips to remember:

1. There are many ways to prove additional time in business. Were you the manager of a similar operation? Were you a minority partner who bought out the other partners? Did you work in the family business for years, but just take it over? Did you sell a similar business and start a new one? **Key point:** *If you were a manager of another firm, did you have check signing authority?*

2. If you need more money than your time in business will warrant to one lender, you may want to work with a broker. They have the flexibility to split the transaction into several parts. They will disclose this to each lender but the risk will be mitigated.

3. If you can show (on paper) how this equipment acquisition is not adversely affecting your monthly cash flow but rather replacing other expenses, the

lender is more likely to approve the transaction. Example: Let's say you are spending $1,500.00 a month having images scanned by a service bureau, and the lease payments on a scanner you have your eye on is $1,100 a month. Let your lender know when you submit your application, and supply copies of invoices to justify the greater risk.

SIN #2:
PERSONAL CREDIT OF THE OWNERS

For most closely held business, whether a corporation, proprietorship, or partnership, the personal credit of the owners is a key factor in deciding whether or not to extend credit. Remember, you are the business!

- Get a copy of your credit report from each of the three major reporting agencies: Equifax (800) 685-1111, Experian (formerly TRW), (888) 397-3742, and Trans Union (800) 888-4213 before you apply for credit. There may be errors in the report that you can have corrected before you apply. It may be possible to get negative items removed even if they are correct!

- If a lien or judgment has been filed against you, it becomes a matter of public record, and will appear on your credit report. If you have satisfied the lien or judgment, it is **your** responsibility to notify the reporting agencies in writing so that the item will be reported as being satisfied.

- If you have ever had a debt placed for collection, advise your lender at the time of your request. If it was paid, be prepared to show proof. If it was not paid, you will need to pay it or explain why.

- If you have outstanding tax liens or defaulted student loans, get them cleared up before you even try to get financing.

SIN #3:

NOT CARRYING ADEQUATE BANK BALANCES

Lenders vary a great deal on what they consider an adequate bank balance for the size transaction requested. They all agree, however, that a certain minimum cash flow through the BUSINESS checking account is necessary to support the additional debt. It is imperative to have a business checking account no matter how small your business is.

- If you are a proprietorship it may be possible to combine your business and personal checking account to show a greater average daily balance.

- Your business bank account is one of the best ways to establish time in business. As soon as you have a company name open your account. Your doors may not be open, but your business is!

- If you have more than one business account, list them ALL, including any business money market or savings accounts.

SIN #4:
"SHOT GUNNING" YOUR CREDIT REQUEST

Many business owners, not understanding the credit industry, will complete and submit several credit applications. The very <u>first</u> thing every lender does is to pull a credit report on the principals of the business. These multiple "hits" on the credit reports of the owners can be the kiss of death to a marginal applicant, and adversely affect even the best credit risk. The "green eye shade" people don't know if you are trying to get $50,000 from several sources (50+50+50= 150) or if the other companies have turned you down. Either scenario is not good and will require extensive explanations.

- If you want to get several quotes, that's fine; but only complete and submit one credit application. If you chose to use a leasing broker, they have the ability to shop the credit markets on your behalf without tracking up your credit.

SIN #5:
NOT SUBMITTING ACCURATE DATA

In today's "information society" seldom do the applicant and the financing source meet face to face. Sloppy or omitted information can reap havoc and cause delays with a credit request. Robert Bell and Bob Bell are not necessarily the same person nor is Robert Bell, Jr. the same as Robert Bell. Additionally, Bob Bell's Studio, Inc. is not the same as Bob Bell's Photography.

- **Tip:** Most requests for financing under $75,000 only require a credit application. Take an extra five minutes and fill it out completely and accurately. Here are a few hints.
  1. The exact corporate name and/or dba (doing business as) name: ILA Investments, Inc. dba Independent Leasing Associates
  2. Time in business under current ownership. 18 months is not two years.
  3. Exact street address, not Lakeland Plaza Shopping Center.
  4. All business references with correct account #'s, phone #, and contact name.
  5. Exact legal name of all owners, home addresses, SS#, and % of ownership.
  6. Equipment list as detailed as possible
  7. Name, address, and phone # of the vendor, along with a contact name.
  8. Is the equipment new or used? If used how old?
  9. Prior banks if you have them.
  10. Corporate structure: Corporation, Partnership, LLC, or Proprietorship

SIN #6:
TRYING TO HIDE "STUFF"

Everybody has flaws. It may be a bill that was disputed, a tax lien filed, or a problem arising from a divorce. Ninety nine times out of a hundred lenders will find out about the problem. The best bet is to address it up front, come clean, and tell it all. The truth shall set you free!

- Find an individual at a funding source you are comfortable with. Your vendor may have someone who they have worked with and can help you. Explain the problem and how you resolved it or why it was not resolved. Don't be embarrassed. Lenders have heard every "the dog ate my homework" story you can imagine. Remember, lenders are in business to **approve** transactions, not turn them down. That's how they earn their living!

SIN #7:

HAVING THE WRONG KIND OF DEBT

Every trip to the mailbox yields another great offer for a cheap rate credit card. Because it is so easy to get credit cards many small business owners have resorted to financing equipment using them. In the equipment finance industry there are several types of debt, some good and some bad. Mortgage debt, no matter how large, is fine as long as you are paying it on time. Installment debt; such as cars, loans, leases, are fine also. Revolving debt (credit cards, department store, and gas cards), is a horse of a different color. It's not only how much you have (when the total goes above $25,000 lenders get nervous), but also how much more is available. It may seem crazy but you are better off with $10,000 of credit card debt and $10,000 still available than with the same amount of debt with only a few thousand more available. Go figure! Many of the declines lenders see today are due to excessive credit card debt or the applicants are maxed out on their cards.

- Reduce your revolving debt as quickly as possible or try to convert it into a bank loan.

LET THE BUYER BEWARE!

Every industry has its shady characters. When it comes to money they come out of the woodwork in droves. So it is no surprise there are some unscrupulous players in the equipment leasing and financing industry. The vast majority of the companies you will deal with are straight shooters and ethical, but there are just enough of the shady ones out there that you need to keep your eyes and ears open. Paying for your equipment as it produces revenue can make good business sense if it improves your cash flow and provides tax benefits. However, you should be alert to several potential problems when it comes to financing your equipment. Here are some of Bob Bell's tips:

Know whom you are dealing with! If the equipment vendor recommends someone, ask him or her how many years they have been doing business with this person or company. Don't be ashamed to ask the leasing company for photography references. If the vendor gives you two or three names of leasing companies, they are not doing you a favor. Each firm will "run your credit" and complicate and delay the ultimate approval. It is fine to get more than one quote, but do not complete more than one credit application. If they won't give you an approximate quote without a credit application, beware.

What are the credentials of the person you are dealing with? How long have they been in the leasing and financing business? Do they own the company? Do they have credentials such as CPA (Certified Public Accountant) or CLP (Certified Lease Professional), or CFA (Chartered Financial Analyst)?

Beware of pre-approvals. This is one of Bob's biggest pet peeves—*There Is No Such Thing As Being Pre-Approved*! You will still have to go through the credit review and qualification process. It is simply a marketing ploy to get you to call them. It's about as valid as saying you're pre-approved for your Master of Photography degree!

Are they asking for money up front? Every business operates under different rules. If a leasing company is asking for money "up front" to process your application, you should check them out. Most non-financial statement requests should not require up front fees.

Is the approval in writing: If you don't know the people you are dealing with, ask for a written approval outlining all the terms and conditions of the lease. The written approval should contain the dollar amount of the approval, the term (# of months), the number of advance payments and or security deposits, the end of lease purchase option, the required guarantors, the monthly payment, and/or any other contingencies that must be met. An officer of the company should sign it.

Do they understand the imaging industry? Every industry, including photography, has its quirks. Does your money source understand your business? Do terms such as fire wire, dye sub, or pixel mean anything to them? Recently, Bob was asked to refinance four airplanes. "I know nothing about airplanes so I sent them to a friend of mine who does nothing but airplanes". Will they include a lot of the soft costs such as software, freight, training, and installation in the transaction? If not, maybe you should look elsewhere. Additionally, because the photography industry is unique and changing, they should have special programs, both internally and externally, to address these issues.

Examine the documents before you sign. The document you sign is the **ONLY** thing that counts. Any statements made by sales reps or loan officers are worthless. Below Mr. Bell lists several of the most important items you should look at and question prior to signing any document. Many of you will want your attorney to examine the document for you, and that's a good idea. Be aware, however, that most financial institutions will not alter their documents unless the transaction is over a million dollars. Every change your attorney makes has to be reviewed by the lending institution's attorney also, which can become very expensive.

KEY LENDING TERMS

Default: What are the instances of default? How are they cured? Most documents will specifically state events of default such as late payments or non-payments of amounts due. Beware of certain clauses inserted in some documents that can be deadly.

Set-Off. This is where a financial institution can take money from **ANY** non-trust account you have with them to pay your loan or lease (including joint checking accounts you have with your kids). This is most common in loan agreements and is not usually found in lease documents, as you normally don't have checking and saving accounts with your leasing company.

Adverse Change: This means that if the financial institution even "thinks" you cannot continue to make payments they can accelerate the indebtedness. This is also known as "calling the loan", collecting the remaining payments at one time. Let's say you had a portrait studio and were making your payments as agreed, but a new Wal-Mart is opening down the road with a portrait studio. Your lender could feel threatened and call the loan.

Default in Favor of Third Party: This means if you are in default of another lease or loan, even if it is to an unrelated institution, you are in default on this transaction.

Ratios: If your lender is requiring financial statements to complete the transaction, they will most likely require that you furnish new ones annually. If the new statements don't meet certain financial ratios they may be able to accelerate the indebtedness.

Purchase Option: This is where a lease differs from a loan. A loan is usually made to the business with the equipment as collateral (often it is more than just the equipment you are financing. See blanket lien). In a lease the equipment is sold to the lessor, and you make payments on it for a fixed term. Consequently, it is *most* important that you have a separate piece of paper called an "end of lease purchase option", outlining what happens at the end of the lease term.

Blanket liens: This is another area where leases and loans are different. Most leases only file a lien on the equipment being financed. Most loans, however, file a "blanket lien" which not only covers the equipment you are getting, but any other equipment not covered by a previous filing, AND any equipment you might want to acquire in the future. You may actually have to get the bank's permission to get new equipment! You have technically taken on a silent partner with veto power.

Continuing Guarantee: Be cognizant of the fact that if you have ever signed a personal guarantee with the bank it is most likely a continuing guarantee. This means any other loan you may take out at that bank is guaranteed by you personally.

Late Fees: Every lending institution has them. Just be aware that they are stiff by design.

Grace Period: This is the length of time you have from the date your payment is due until the late fees are imposed. Also, be aware that late fees can be deducted from your security deposit.

Interim Rent: This is an amount of daily accrual between the days your lease is funded until your next scheduled payment is due. None of the payment is used to reduce your outstanding balance. This can be good if it is just a few days and it allows you to better balance your cash flow. It is onerous if it goes over two weeks.

Doc Fees: These are fees you are charged for processing the paperwork and filing the necessary legal documents. They can run from a few dollars to over a thousand.

Delivery and Acceptance: This is the document that says the equipment has been delivered and is in good working order. Technically you should not sign this until the equipment has been delivered and is in proper working order. The reality is every reputable leasing company has a verbal conversation with the signor of the lease or their designee. This covers the terms and condition of what you have signed. It is only then that the lender will disperse funds to the vendors. This is for your protection as well as theirs.

Personal Guarantee: This is where you as an owner of the business agree to make the payments even if the business cannot. Unless you are a fairly large, well-established company with diversified ownership, plan on personally guaranteeing the loan or lease.

Holiday and Vacation Clubs: Having Endless Cash

Growing up I remember when banks offered Christmas and Vacation Club Accounts. These accounts were set up like an installment loan—complete with coupons. Each week I would go to the bank (sorry, no ATM's) and deposit the coupon amount. One account matured in May just in time for summer vacations and the other in November in time for holiday shopping. Although the interest rates were minimal, the accounts were still popular because of their "forced savings" structure.

ARE YOU SALES RICH AND CASH POOR?

What does this have to do with photography you ask? Everything! Managing cash flow is one of the biggest challenges each of us faces as a business owner. I often see clients who can't understand why they don't have any cash, even though they are reaching their sales goals. This is particularly evident during the winter months when revenue is slow. Photographers have trouble paying lab and album bills, rent and payroll. If equipment breaks, there is no money in the checking account to fix it or buy new equipment. Some photographers try to resolve their dilemma by borrowing money from banks or using their credit cards, often paying double-digit interest for the privilege. If you are reaching your sales goals and have control over your expenses, there is virtually no reason for you to borrow money to cover your operating expenses and most of your capital expenses.

Fortunately, in today's era of ATM machines and web-based banking, it is easier to manage your cash, without borrowing money.

TIMING IS EVERYTHING

Cash flow problems often occur because of a mismatch in timing from when you take money in and pay it out. For example, your rent/mortgage payment is the same in February and March when cash is tight as it is in September and October when your revenue is coming in. Another example is lab and album expenses—the bulk of the expenses for the weddings you photograph in October may not occur until January or February when the order is placed and fulfilled. This problem is not unique to photographers, many businesses face similar timing issues. Cash management is both the process of saving money for and maximizing our return on idle liquid assets.

SPECIALIZED SAVINGS ACCOUNTS TO THE RESCUE

Since we have little control over when people will need our services or when expenses, like rent are due, we need to set aside money when we have it, for a time in the future when we'll need it. In other words, cash management. While most banks offer cash management services to commercial clients, the fees and minimum balances usually required for such a service make it impractical for micro-businesses, such as photographers. However, there is hope—specialized savings accounts to the rescue!

Specialized savings accounts are modern day club accounts. Money is set-aside for a specific purpose or expense we know will occur in the future. I prefer to have lots of accounts for each of my major expense categories (you really can't have too many savings accounts).

HERE'S HOW IT WORKS

Let's look at cost of goods sold (lab fees, album costs, film, etc.). Cost of goods sold is an expense that is directly related to sales; that is, without sales, there would be no expense. Let us suppose that based on prior years' records you have determined that CGS is 25% of total sales. (For example your total CGS is $25,000 and total sales is $100,000. Twenty-five divided by 100 is 25%). To ensure you always have enough money for these expenses, establish a separate savings account designated for this purpose. For every dollar in sales you take in, you should transfer twenty-five cents into this account. When a Cost of Goods Sold bill comes in, you simply transfer the money back to your checking account to cover the expense. While this might seem like a lot of work, it is quite simple. At the end of each day or week determine your total sales, multiply by the appropriate percentage and make the transfer. This is why having an ATM card, web-based banking, or telephone access greatly simplifies the process.

Equipment repair and purchase is another candidate for specialized savings accounts. With digital technology changing almost daily, it is imperative that we set aside money to keep pace with technology. The first step is to determine, on average, how much money you plan to spend for new equipment and repairs. Let us assume it is $6,000 per year (or $500 per month). Again, establish a savings or money-market account specifically for this purpose. Ask your bank to automatically withdraw $500 each month from your *main checking* account into this new account. (This is usually a FREE service offered by financial institutions.) You don't have to think about it at all, it is done automatically. What could be simpler? Each time you make an equipment purchase or repair, transfer the money back to your main checking account.

This process is known as re-capitalization. Lucrative business owners understand the importance of continuously putting money aside to re-capitalize their business. By identifying your long-term, big-ticket equipment needs (capital purchases) you can set aside a *fixed amount of money each month* to replace and repair your equipment as needed. The use of putting a fixed amount of money away each month evens out your cash flow on a month-to-month basis. In addition, large purchases for items such as computers and digital cameras are withdrawn from this special account and have *no impact on your day-to-day cash flow.*

It is not always practical or preferable to pay cash for a purchase (such as a car). Let's assume your car payment/lease is $350 per month. In addition, car maintenance is another $150 per month. In this example you would set aside $500 per month in your specialized account. All of your loan or lease payments plus maintenance would come out of this account. But what happens when you pay off the loan? Do you lower the transfer amount or keep it the same? *You should keep it the same!* Why? Because after the loan is paid off you will eventually need to replace the car with another one. By continuing to make deposits into this account you are ensured of having the needed cash to make your down payment on your next car.

THE CHOICE IS YOURS

The above examples illustrate the two basic methods available for establishing specialized savings accounts. Each method has its pluses and minuses. In the first example, you determine the expense's relationship to total sales and make the funds transfer yourself. The advantage: you transfer money only when you have an actual cash sale, which increases the likelihood that money exists for the transfer. The disadvantage, it is a manual system, and you can forget to follow through.

The second example has the bank make automatic monthly transfers from one account to the other. By automating the process, you dramatically increase the chance of the program being implemented. The down side, you will need to have the cash in the account in order for the transfer to be made.

I recommend using a combination of both. For expenses, that occur frequently (like Cost of Goods Sold), the manual process of regularly sweeping money between accounts tends to work best. For annual or infrequent expenses (like equipment purchases), the automatic transfer method is preferable.

While you're at it, consider establishing specialized savings accounts for other expenses such as automobile purchase and repairs, education and seminars, retirement contributions, estimated income taxes, and of course—vacations.

> *Note: It is important to remember that the primary purpose for these specialized savings accounts is not for the interest you will earn, rather it is to have the needed funds available to you when you need them. However, interest rates should not be ignored. If you notice an account always has a balance of at least $5,000, you may want to consider having $5,000 in a short-term Certificate of Deposit (CD) that will earn you a higher rate of return. In addition, using money market accounts instead of savings accounts can also improve your investment results. As always, you should seek the advice of qualified advisors such as your CPA, financial planner, or banker.*

Lucrative Pricing Strategies

THE ART OF PRICING

One of the most common questions I am asked, as a consultant, is, "How much should I charge?" The question appears to be asked in such away that the answer is akin to finding the Holy Grail.

Unfortunately there is no magic formula. On a basic level, price is based on your expenses plus your desired profit. However, logical pricing is not always the smartest practice. It is important for photographers to understand not only the mathematics of pricing but also the psychology of pricing, as well. Lucrative pricing is as much an art as it is a science.

DO YOUR PRICES COMMAND RESPECT?

The easiest way for me to explain this concept is by example. My parents had just redone our home including the kitchen. My father placed an ad in the local paper to sell the old stove and asked a modest amount: $50 or best offer, just to get rid of it. No one called, so he decided to place another ad and this time asked $250. The stove sold within a week. What changed? It wasn't the stove; it was the public's *perception* of the stove. At $50 the stove was a great deal; however, the low price also made it appear as though it was damaged goods.

By comparison, the more expensive and rare an item is, the greater it's perceived value. Consider Hasselblad cameras. Certainly it is one of the finest cameras on the market. Is it the best camera? Maybe. But look how it is priced, at the top of the market. Photographers perceive Hasselblad to be the best. At trade shows, I've seen photographers line up 5-10 people deep to see what Hasselblad equipment they can spend their money on. Are people lining up to spend money with you? If not, your problem may not be that your prices are too high, rather it may be that they are too low.

DECIDE WHICH END OF THE MARKET YOU WANT TO SERVE

If I were to ask you what is the first thing that comes to mind when I say, "Red Roof Inn, Comfort Inn, or Motel Six," what would you say? You would probably say, cheap, inexpensive, or something along this line. On the other hand, if I said, "Ritz Carlton or the Four Seasons Hotel," you might say luxurious, expensive, elegant, etc.

Both examples are from the same industry, yet they serve vastly different markets. The former treats their product as if it was a commodity and the latter as a premium service that people aspire to have.

While the above example is a little extreme, it is representative of a trend in the market place, the polarization of the goods and services. With the size of the middle-class shrinking in our society, so has the market for middle-end products and services. The purchasing habits of the public are changing, people either want something quick and inexpensive, or they will indulge themselves with some of life's finer pleasures.[26]

Let's look at the restaurant business: There are fast food chains and just above them family restaurants. There is not much else until you get to the luxury fare. What I have noticed is that there are large mass-market merchants on one end and boutique premium merchants on the other end. The problem is the gap in the middle.

For those of you who still have reservations about this concept, think about the following industries: lumber yards, hardware stores, office and stationary supplies, toy stores, eye glasses, bookstores, restaurants, dental care, and to a some degree, medical care. In each of these professions, independent (mom and pop) stores ruled the landscape until large mass merchants transformed the product or service into a commodity. Yet, some independent companies have not only survived, they have also thrived. They succeeded not by trying to compete with the mass marketers, but by serving those clients whose needs weren't being met, those who still wanted a premium product or service.

Of all the pricing examples I use, this is one of the hardest for many photographers to grasp. If you are priced in the middle, you may be too expensive for value-oriented clients, and you're not perceived to be good enough for the premium clients. People often mistake my statements, as meaning that they should

---

[26] *Clicking, 17 Trends That Drive Your Business And Your Life*, Faith Popcorn and Lys Marigold, ©1997 Harper Business

either be the cheapest or the most expensive photographer in their area. Others argue that the middle of the market is the largest segment. Although I can't point to any particular study, my experience indicates that the gap between commodity and premium products is greater in large urban areas than it is in rural areas. However, the principle behind this pricing concept is the same regardless of where you are located. When creating a price list, think of who your target audience is, and direct your prices toward them. It's like the old joke; a person walks into a store and says to the salesperson, "I want something good and cheap." The salesperson replies, "Make up your mind, you can't have both."

ARE YOUR CLIENTS PAYING
FOR PIECES OF PAPER OR FOR YOUR EXPERIENCE?

One of my favorite stories on the subject of pricing comes from a book by Harry Beckwith entitled: *Selling The Invisible*. In it, Mr. Beckwith recounts this story about Picasso. One day while painting in Paris, Picasso was approached by a woman who said it was her dream to have him do a drawing of her and asked him if he would oblige. He agreed and he picked up a new canvas and began to sketch a drawing of the woman. After about 20 minutes or so, he said he was done and turned the canvas around to the woman. The woman could not believe her eyes at how beautiful the drawing of her looked. She told him she was thrilled and asked him how much she owed him. Picasso responded, "5,000 francs." The woman was horrified. "5,000 francs for 20 minutes for your time?" Picasso replied, "No, for a lifetime worth of experience."

In the long run, you may find you can charge a lot more for your experience than you can for your time or pieces of paper.

DON'T DEFEND YOUR PRICE; EMPHASIZE YOUR ADDED VALUE.

If you walk into a Mercedes dealership, do you think they will defend the price of the car or emphasize the value and benefits of owning a Mercedes? They know they are selling more than a car; they are selling prestige, luxury, and style. If you have to ask the price, you're not a Mercedes type of client.

It is tempting for us as photographers to get caught up in the numbers game with our prospective clients, especially when, "How much are your packages?" is one of the first questions they ask. However, when you defend your prices it makes you look as if you don't think you are worth what you're asking, and all you are offering are pieces of paper. When you emphasize value and emotion, the images you create are priceless.

When clients ask you about your prices, don't get mad or defensive. Instead, review all the *added* (unique) benefits they will receive for being one of your clients. It is not enough for the benefits to be unique; the prospect must *perceive the benefit to be of value to them.* For example, suppose you inform your prospect that you can deliver the finished portrait the same day you take the image. If the person is looking for a professional business portrait, speed of delivery may be an important in their decision process. However, if it is for a 24x30 family portrait they've been saving for, turnaround time may be less important.

Maximize Your Profitability

People are often motivated to purchase photography for the memories you capture for them. Have prospects talk about how they will feel on the day of the wedding, or tell you a story about their grandmother in the old faded photograph to be restored. I remember working with the parents of the bride to design their album after the wedding. They were "complaining" about how much everything (not just photography) cost. Should they add more photographs, take some out, etc. I asked the mother of the bride to tell me what she was feeling in several of the photographs in question. She spent the next half-hour telling me in great detail all the joy and emotion she felt. Price was no longer an issue; preserving those precious memories was all that mattered.

The more you can connect with your clients on an emotional level, the greater their *perceived value* of the added benefits you offer the less sensitive they will be to price. Kirsten Snow (Art Leather/GNP) summed it best when she told me, "You have to go through the heart, to get to the wallet." Nowhere is this truer than with photography.

PRICE IS RARELY AN EFFECTIVE USP

Read through the newspaper on any given Sunday and you are bound to see an ad from Sears, JC Penney, Wal-Mart, or Olin Mills for a family portrait. For less than $10 you can get up to 100 pieces of paper with an image on it. For most photographers, it costs more than $10 to proof a roll of film. How can we possibly compete against this?

The Lucrative Photographer

Too often we let companies such as these dictate how we operate our business. It is no surprise that consumers become trained to look for how many pieces of paper one studio offers versus another. This leads studios to feel that in order to compete they must offer even more images at even lower prices.

When you use price as your main selling feature, there is almost always someone who is willing to match or beat your price. It is rarely a battle you can win. Emphasizing price only serves to undermine your ability to distinguish yourself from your competitors and makes price the main factor in how people chose their photographer.

CHANGE THE RULES

A simple rule to follow is, if you can't compete on your competitor's terms, make them compete on yours. You want prospects to make a decision on something that plays to *your strengths* and your *competitors' weaknesses*. As independent photographers there is no way you can compete based on price, nor should you. Emphasize the areas where you have a clear competitive advantage. For example, if you handprint your photographs and your competition uses a machine print, that can be a competitive advantage. When prospects leaves your studio, *they will ask* the next photographer if they handprint their photographs. If this competitive advantage is also important to the prospect, you significantly increase your chances of gaining a new client.

Maximize Your Profitability

DON'T CHARGE LESS—OFFER MORE

Studios competing on price are usually not very flexible in what they offer or how they deliver it. This is one of the reasons why they can afford to have lower prices. Look for products and services that have a *high-perceived value* to your client and a *low cost* to your studio. Complimentary retouching of all images, special premiums or programs for your best clients, or home installation of your client's wall portrait are just a few examples of services you can offer your clients without cutting into your profitability. Look for ways to create an experience your clients would pay for, in and of itself.

HIGH PRICES CAN BE AN ADVANTAGE

Being on the high end of the price scale has its own advantages. High priced products offer prestige. High-priced products and services are perceived as being a superior choice—whether or not this is actually the case. However, you should be able to back up the higher price with a quality product and exceptional service.

Price will be a deciding factor if the consumer cannot distinguish the difference between what you offer versus your competition. However, if what you offer is *significantly different* from your competition many consumers are willing to pay a little extra. The greater the perceived difference, the greater the relative value the product or service has—a much more lucrative strategy.

The Lucrative Photographer

ARE YOU READY FOR PRIME-TIME

As the new millennium approached, people began to make plans for the big New Year's Celebration. Out of curiosity, I called a few restaurants and hotels and asked them what their New Year's Eve packages were going for. I received quotes from as little as $600 to over $1,500 per person (The Ritz Carlton had a *$100,000* package that was sold out a year prior to the holiday). New Year's Eve has always carried a premium price tag and people don't seem to mind; after all, it's a once in a millennium event.

Premium or Prime Time pricing is prevalent throughout our country. Airlines, hotel, and phone companies all charge more for their services during peak/normal business hours. Vacation resorts charge a premium during peak holidays as well. It even costs more to go the movies at night than during the day, and you can't use your discount tickets during the first two weeks a movie opens. Yet where is the public outrage? There is none because the public understands why businesses do this, and they have come to accept it. Yet Prime Time pricing is virtually nowhere to be found in photography.

In 1995, the PPA commissioned the Winfield Group to do market research for its members. The report asked what the most convenient time/days the public would prefer to have family portraits taken. The most convenient time (50% of those responding) to have a portrait done during the week was after work and 75% of respondents preferred their portraits to be done on the weekend.[27] I'm sure the results of this survey are not a surprise to most of us. However, my research has found very few photographers who have taken advantage by charging either a premium or have a higher minimum for peak portrait times.

The same is true for weddings. In New England, most weddings take place May through October. The most popular time to have a wedding is Saturday night. Ask any reception facility, and I'm sure the minimum for a Saturday night in June is significantly higher than a Friday night in January. Yet most photographers charge the same regardless of when the wedding takes place.

MORE MONEY AND BETTER HOURS

The combination of the public's willingness to pay a premium for peak times and their desire to have photographs taken at peak times is a potential financial windfall for all photographers. While people will continue to get married on the dates *they* want, you have the ability to charge significantly more for the peak dates with the same amount of effort. Hotels, caterers, florists, and bands do, so why don't photographers? If your studio does more than one wedding per day, consider charging a premium for evening weddings versus day weddings. (Another common practice in the catering business.) Also consider charging more for yourself versus one of your staff.

---

[27] *A Market Research Report For The Members Of The Professional Photographers Of America, Inc.*, ©1995 The Winfield Group, Atlanta, Georgia. For a copy contact the PPA at (404) 522-8600.

The Lucrative Photographer

With respect to family portraits, most clients have a little flexibility with their schedules. Use of Prime Time pricing will encourage some of your clients to have their portraits done on Tuesday afternoon at 1:00 versus Saturday at 10:00. If not, you'll be well compensated.

YOUR PERSONAL TIME IS IMPORTANT TOO!

What is time with your family worth to you? If you want to spend time with your family on Saturday or Sunday, how much would you need to earn in order to make it worth time away from the ones you love? Photographers forget that serving their clients at night and on the weekend has its price. The premium you charge should be enough to compensate you for your sacrifice!

This practice even applies to initial consultations. We have all had a prospective client want to meet with us on a Saturday only to cancel at the last minute or not show up at all, and those that do show up, rarely hire you.

People won't respect your time if you don't either. When people call and ask to set up a Saturday appointment (for a non portrait sitting occasion) I politely explain that I photograph weddings and portraits on the weekends and if I don't have any sessions, I have made a promise to my family to spend that free time with them.

Nine out of ten people immediately understand what I am saying and try to arrange an appointment for during the week. However, there are those who insist

119

upon seeing me anyway. What I have learned to say is: "If you like I can give you my wife's work phone number. If she says it is ok for me to spend time with you and not her on the weekend, I will gladly to set up an appointment with you." No one has ever asked for her number.

Most photographers say they don't spend enough time with their family and friends. In order to change this, you need to re-establish your priorities. Remember, how you spend your time in the long run, says a lot about what is truly important to you.

BUT WON'T I LOSE CLIENTS?

This is a common myth. Sure there will be a few people who will object to paying a premium for peak times, but they are the same people who won't spend a lot of money with you anyway. Let them go to someone else. If you're indispensable to your clients, they won't mind the premium price. I know of several photographers (myself included) for whom brides changed their wedding dates to accommodate the photographer's schedule. I'm sure the same is true for those of you who do family portraits. Clients will pay the premium because, in their mind, there is only one choice for a photographer. To quote fellow photographer Darton Drake, "No photographer has ever gone out of business by charging too much, yet many have by not charging enough." If you are well entrenched with your target audience you have nothing to worry about. If not, your problem is most likely the result of being poorly niched and lacking an effective marketing strategy. However, I believe there is a huge potential windfall awaiting each and every one of us.

The Lucrative Photographer

PROFESSIONAL SERVICES NEVER GO ON SALE

Would you make an appointment to see a doctor who is having a sale on a medical procedure? I doubt it. The same can be said of accountants, lawyers, and most other professionals.

The public views professional services differently from a retail operation. Retail stores carry merchandise that can be sold to anyone. Professional services are individually tailored to each client. You hire a professional at a time you need his or her services, not because they have decided to have a sale.

Are you really going to change your plans to have a cavity filled at a dentist's office because the next week they're having a 50% off sale? What does having a sale say about the quality of his/her skills as a doctor?

It is important for us as photographers to remember that although the result of our efforts is a product, people hire us for our professional skills. To be treated as professionals, we must price ourselves as professionals.

PROMOTIONS REALLY DON'T WORK

While sales and promotions have the short-term effect of increasing volume, it comes at the expense of your studio's profitability and once the promotion is over, so is the increase in activity. Clients who come in *only for the specials* are price sensitive. If someone offers a better special they are likely to leave and take their business. Surprisingly, studies have shown that many of the people you are attracting into your studio at discounted prices are the same people who would normally pay your regular prices. This is not to say that you should not use promotions or specials. I have long maintained that these are the only two groups of clients where this strategy can work: First, for new prospects to introduce them to your studio, and second, to reward your very best clients for their patronage. Anything else and you're just taking away your profits.

In creating specials and promotions, NEVER put on sale a product or service your clients would buy anyway. To do so is tantamount to throwing money away. Let me explain by way of example. One June I called my local camera supply store to buy film. When I buy film, I don't ask if they are having a sale, I need it in order to earn my living. Yet this store decided to put film on sale during the peak wedding season. For every "X" number of rolls I purchased I received so many for free. Where's the logic? It would make more sense for the store to offer me an incentive to buy a higher profit margin item if I purchased more than "X" dollars worth of film.

The photography industry is not alone in making these types of mistakes. I was fortunate enough to have tickets to the 1999 baseball All-Star game. The day of the game I walked into a sports store in downtown Boston (where the game was played), and they had the official All-Star baseball on sale for 30% off the regular price. Why? I would have bought the ball at the regular price; I was going to the game. They simply gave away money they didn't need to.

PRICES BASED ON REALITY

Photographers seem to have a mortal fear that if people know how much it will really cost to use their services, people won't hire them. I have never understood the logic of this way of thinking. Would you really hire someone without having any idea of how much you will ultimately spend? How would you feel if you hired a contractor to do work on your house based on a "package" of $5,000, but when the work was complete it cost you $20,000. No one likes surprises. When I first started, I used "low" minimums to entice people to hire us. The biggest complaint we received was that people wanted to know how much it was ultimately going to cost them. It wasn't that they objected to our prices, they just had not prepared themselves for the backend expense. If you're not comfortable with how much you charge, you can't expect your clients to be either.

Your "minimum investment" or "package" should be based on what you need to *at least break-even*. That is, if a client hires you for your minimum, even if they don't spend a single cent more, you would be able to pay for your salary and expenses. Consider spending time with prospects, before they hire you, going over their wish list and how much it will cost. Will you lose a few prospects this way? Probably, but the ones you lose are not your ideal clients anyway. Those who hire you will know they will be making a significant investment with you. This should make you look forward to their session because you know you will be properly compensated.

Maximize Your Profitability

The concept of incentive-based pricing is simple; for just a little more money you get a lot more value. Let me illustrate:

My wife went to have the oil changed in her car and the mechanic informed her that the tires were quite worn and should be replaced. The store gave her three tire options, essentially; good, better, and best. The top of the line tire was considerably more money but the company included value-added services such free tire rotation and free front-end alignments, making the effective difference almost insignificant. In the long run it was actually cheaper to buy the more expensive tires.

Use of incentives makes maintaining profitability easier because clients are given the option to buy more *on top of their regular purchase.* By comparison, when you discount your work, you lessen its value because you are implying to your clients that your work may not be worth its full value. It is critical to remember to offer incentives ONLY when the sale is ABOVE your break-even sales point or preferably, above what your average client purchases. This is a critical point. Why would you want to reward someone who is spending LESS than your average client does?

Incentive-based pricing also gives you an indication of who will spend money and who will not. When people try to haggle with your minimum price, what does this say about how they value what you do? Since we began our studio in 1990, I can count on one hand the number of times a client, who did not take advantage of our incentives, surprised me and spent well above the minimum investment. If the incentives are strong enough, people will take advantage of them. My experience with this program is that people, who take advantage of the incentives, will spend 2-3 times my minimum investment PRIOR to the wedding. No one else in the wedding industry works on speculation, and with proper incentives, neither will you.

Below are samples from our current wedding incentive program. Notice that in each instance, clients are required to *invest in additional product prior to the event* in order to take advantage of the incentive program. I do tell my clients that although I do take an unlimited number of images at each wedding, I do alter my approach based in part on their pre-wedding order. In other words, I am more likely to take a greater number of images for a client who orders a two-volume set plus parent albums than I am from a client who hires me just for my minimum investment. Since clients know this up front, there is no confusion and it encourages them to upgrade the size of their album, purchase individual prints, and add parent albums and wall portraits *prior* to the wedding. Although these examples are from a wedding, you can easily adapt and modify them for whatever type of photography you do.

We have used some form of incentive-based pricing since we opened. As I noted earlier, it is very rare for someone to sign up for only the minimum investment prior to the wedding and then buy out the store afterwards. It just doesn't happen. However, every so often I will come across a photographer who tells me that they have a modest minimum and people are still spending a fortune. Without exception, these people have a very loyal client base, are perceived as indispensable to their clients, and have a strong reputation. They can get away with a low minimum because their clients know in advance what it is going to ultimately cost them, which in reality is the same thing.

WEDDING PRICING INCENTIVES

BRIDE AND GROOM
- Order and Prepay for a large 50 page multi-print album and receive a complimentary full panorama page for your album
- Order and Prepay for a large 60 page multi-print album and receive two complimentary half page panoramas, *plus* a full panorama page for your album
- Order and Prepay for a large two-volume 70 page multi-print library-bound leather album and receive two complimentary half page panoramas, a full panorama page, plus a leather slip case.

FAMILY ALBUMS
- Order and Prepay for a 20 page album and receive four (4) additional album pages
- Order and Prepay for a 30 page album and receive six (6) additional album pages
- Order and Prepay for a 40 page album and receive eight (8) additional album pages
- Order and Prepay for a 50 page album and receive ten (10) additional album pages

WALL PORTRAITS
- Order and Prepay for any wall portrait and receive a $150 credit toward any frame we offer.

It is vital that in creating incentives you price your work with profitably in mind! That is, if you are offering a panorama page as a bonus item, the price of the work the client pays for should include sufficient profit to cover the cost of the panorama and still maintain your needed profit margin. The price of the original product/service is really the price you want to sell both of them for. If your client does not take advantage of any bonus items, your profit margin is that much higher. Before offering any bonus items, review your costs and consider adjusting your current prices to reflect the additional incentives.

SIZE DOESN'T MATTER

Another pricing concept I never fully understood is the logic of why an 8x10 print (that costs only $2 more than a 4x5 to print) should sell for $10-$20 more. It takes the same amount of effort to order either size image, which was created at the same sitting. This is why we adopted our "one-size fits all" approach to pricing. Any photograph 8x10 or smaller sells for the same price. You may be surprised to note that *not once* has a client ever complained or questioned the logic of this pricing structure. When people go on vacation, a common souvenir is a tee shirt. Have you ever noticed that the small tee shirt sells for the same price as the large or even extra large? Even though the larger shirts have more material, the price is the same. People understand this concept and logic behind it. Since we have adopted this pricing concept, we have sold more 4x5 and 5x7 prints than we have 8x10s. People order the size they need, not the size they can afford.

Maximize Your Profitability

The same is true for wall portraits. Virtually every seminar I attend stresses the importance of projecting images to sell the large size images. Are we projecting the images because it is in our clients' best interest or our own? We project because traditionally photographs are priced based on a multiple of cost. It is in our best interest to sell larger images because we make more money. I asked a few lab owners what are the most common size wall portraits they print. The vast majority of all wall portraits are either 20x24 or 24x30 and smaller. As a result we now charge the same amount of money for all wall portraits 20x24 and smaller. Again people are buying 11x14s and 16x20s even though the price is the same.

We use the same strategy for our wedding albums by selling them by the page not by the print. The benefit to the client is it is easy to figure out how much it will cost, and they don't have to eliminate as many images from their album. From our perspective, clients get to put in the number and size photographs they want while they are charged for the most expensive page layout. It is a win-win situation.

Why should your income be tied to the size of the photograph people purchase? As I've stressed throughout this book, you should be compensated based on economic need, talent, and your niche. Size shouldn't matter.

WHAT'S THE RUSH?

Have you ever had a client say they needed an album or photograph in a hurry? In your effort to be nice and accommodating, you most likely did it as a favor for no additional charge, even though your lab or album company charged *you* a premium. Vendors charge a premium for rush orders for a reason; without charging a premium there would be chaos. Production schedules would be impossible to meet. What a rush fee or premium does, is weed out those clients who really don't need the photographs quickly, but who want special treatment nonetheless. Those clients, who truly need a quick turnaround understand the need for a rush charge and will pay the additional price. Others will decide that they can live with the delay. Federal Express created a whole industry based on people who didn't want to wait a few days for regular mail. Has the Post Office or UPS gone out of business? No. You will be surprised to find out how few people really need their photographs yesterday when they have to pay a premium for the privilege. Of course, *on occasion*, it is perfectly permissible to do a favor for one of *your best clients* and not charge a rush fee. However, when you do so, you should let them know that you normally charge a premium for this service and that as a favor, you will make a one-time exception. Having a rush order policy will make your production schedule run smoother and can provide a source of additional revenue from those who positively need it overnight.

USE DISCOUNTS WITH CAUTION

I have long maintained that there are only two groups of people who should receive discounted pricing: first time buyers; as an inducement to become clients and your very best clients, to show your appreciation. Everyone else should pay full retail. This is why you need to know who your target audience is and who it is not. Your pricing and promotions should be structured based on the wants and needs of the top 20% of your client base. Now this doesn't mean that you can't have special promotions or you shouldn't do favors for certain clients. Specials and promotions should be used to thank and reward your best clients by offering them a product or service not available to the general public. Specials can also be a valuable way to introduce your services to first time buyers. (You see this strategy used quite often with magazines. They give first time subscribers a special rate. When your renewal is due, you pay the regular subscription rate.) Ironically, the profitable clients usually require little to no maintenance and are a pleasure to work for. Non-profitable clients are just the opposite. Clients that only hire you when you have a special are not lucrative clients, and in most instances are a drain on your time and cost you money. Lucrative photographers continuously evaluate their clients' profitability, eliminating those that drain profit, replacing them with people who fit their ideal client profile.

SPECIALS VS. LIMITED EDITIONS

A common practice among portrait studios is to offer special theme sets throughout the year as a way to increase the buying frequency of their clients—an excellent idea. However, photographers more often than not offer these promotions at a reduced fee because they feel it is the only way to entice their clients into the studio. While this works well with new and existing clients who are budget conscious, it can have a negative impact on your bottom line. In addition, it trains your clients to wait for the discount. This is exactly what has happened in the pizza industry. When was the last time you paid full price for a pizza? If you're like me, you probably receive several coupons every week in the mail from different restaurants offering some sort of special. The same is true for many retail stores. Companies like Circuit City, Best Buy, Staples, and Office Depot have sales so often one has to wonder if anyone pays full price. What these companies have done, willingly or not, is make what they offer a commodity, where the only difference between companies is who is currently offering the lowest price. While the big companies can afford to play this game (for a little while), as a sole proprietor, it is a recipe for disaster.

A good friend of mine, Nancy Mickel, M.Photog.Cr., owner of *Studio Art Photography* in Oklahoma City, Oklahoma, uses a different strategy in her studio. She creates special sets throughout the year that are available for a limited time. Since it costs her time and money to create these special sets she charges up to two to three times her normal sitting fee for these specials (limited edition) sets. She has established these promotions as a value-added service to be offered to her clients. Nancy has clients calling her all year long asking her when she is going to have these "specials" that they will pay a premium for.

Theme sets are available for a limited time and once the promotion has ended your clients will not have the opportunity to have the *exact* same set again. At a minimum, they will have to wait up to a year before a similar *limited edition set* is offered again. The difference between a special and a limited edition is the former is sold at a discount and the latter sells at a premium. The distinction is very important. Let's suppose your regular session fee is $50. If you have a promotion or special, you might discount your session fee to $25. If you photographed fifty people as part of that promotion the discount represents a $1,250 drop in revenue.

Instead of offering the same old traditional sets, use your imagination to enhance the session, and your clients' experience, by creating a limited edition set you can charge a premium for. Instead of discounting the session by $25 suppose you add $25 ($75 per session). This simple change in philosophy in this example would generate an additional $2,500 in revenue (see chart below). If you offered only four limited edition sessions each year (and many studios have more) you would generate over $10,000 in increased revenue ($2,500 x four session) with no offsetting expense, in other words, the extra cash is yours!

LIMITED EDITIONS VS DISCOUNT SESSIONS			
	Regular Session	Discount Session	Limited Edition
Sitting Fee	$50	$25	$75
Number of Sessions	50	50	50
Session Income	$2,500	$1,250	$3,750

Besides just the dollars involved, think about the type of client a limited edition session attracts versus clients attracted to the discounted sessions. People who purchase a limited edition portrait place a premium value on the quality of work you create, while the others are motivated by the discount. Which of these two types of clients would you prefer to do business with?

Limited editions need not be restricted to special sets. Why not offer a special type of framed portraits (such as a deckled edge watercolor print) or services that are not available at other times throughout the year.

Astute business owners have long recognize that limited editions are a way of attracting attention to their businesses when people might not have otherwise done so, *without having to offer a sale*. For your next promotion, consider raising your fee for a limited edition setting.

PROMOTE YOUR EVERY DAY PRICE
A great place to learn about marketing and pricing is the Sunday newspaper ads. Every week I see ads promoting product after product as if they were on sale, but they're not. When people see a product advertised in a flyer, they assume that it is on sale. (At the least the flyer sparks their interest.) For your next promotion, don't lower your price; instead promote the product at your regular price! You'll still attract clients and money you can take to the bank.

IMPACT AND CONSEQUENCES
It is important to consider the consequences of your pricing strategy. While a sound strategy can be extremely lucrative, the opposite can be detrimental. Is your pricing strategy designed to appeal to your ideal target audience or is it attracting price shoppers and those clients trying to get the "best deal"?

Maximize Your Profitability

Consider the following example: A photographer advertises that if you hire him/her within seven days of the initial appointment you get to keep the proofs for free. The logic is since the proofs are already paid for it doesn't cost any money to give the proofs away. Will this type of incentive increase bookings? Absolutely, but what type of client do you think this strategy attracts? What message does it convey about the value of the proofs?

Imagine if you and every other photographer in your area decided to match this offer. The public will assume the proofs are automatically theirs to keep. Now, instead of being an incentive, it becomes a standard of doing business. (Sound familiar?) To entice new clients, you will have to offer even more for free and say "so long" to your profitability. Is this far fetched? Look at supermarkets. One store came up with the idea of offering double coupons and now it is the norm with most stores. The same is true with credit card companies and air mileage. Once it becomes the norm, it is difficult to take it away without having a negative impact on your sales.

By comparison, what if the price of the proofs was based on how much a person invested in your services *prior* to the portrait or wedding? It says the proofs have real value. Even if other photographers adopt a similar policy your profitability is still intact. In creating a price list, think of the long-term impact the policy will have on your business. Remember that it is always easier to lower prices than it is to raise them.

The Lucrative Photographer

The point I want to stress is for you to look beyond today's dollar. It is very tempting at times (particularly when you're starting out) to want to bring in *anyone* who is willing to say yes regardless of price or profit. However, whom you do business with today, effects whom you will do business with tomorrow and in the future. Choose wisely.

RESOURCES

BOOKS

Selling The Invisible: A Field Guide To Modern Marketing, ©1997, Harry Beckwith, Warner Books.

Price Wars: How To Win The Battle For Your Customers, ©1994, Thomas J. Winninger, St. Thomas Press, 800-899-8971.

The Strategy And Tactics Of Pricing: A Guide To Profitable Decision Making, ©1995 & 1987, Thomas T. Nagle and Reek K. Holden, Prentice-Hall, Inc.

Priced To Sell: The Complete Guide To More Profitable Pricing, ©1996, Herman Holtz, Upstart Publishing Company.

Clicking, 17 Trends That Drive Your Business And Your Life, Faith Popcorn and Lys Marigold, ©1997, Harper Business

Maximize Your Profitability

CONSULTANTS

Paresky Flitt & Company—14 W Plain St, Wayland, MA 01778-4475, 508-650-1122, www.pareskyflitt.com

Independent Leasing Associates—Bob Bell can be contacted at bob@independentleasing.com, by phone at 800-685-7571 or www.independentleasing.com

SOFTWARE

Quicken/QuickBooks—Intuit, Inc., 2535 Garcia Avenue, Mountain View, California 94043, 800-446-8848, www.intuit.com

Microsoft Money—Microsoft Corp., One Microsoft Way, Redmond, Washington, 98052-6399, 425-882-8080, www.microsoft.com

REPORTS

A Market Research Report For The Members Of The Professional Photographers Of America, Inc., ©1995 The Winfield Group, Atlanta, Georgia. For a copy of the report, contact the PPA (404) 522-8600.

Marketing and Sales

- ☞ DEVELOP A WRITTEN MARKETING PLAN
- ☞ WHAT IS THE LIFETIME VALUE OF YOUR CLIENTS
- ☞ CLIENT RETENTION: THE LIFEBLOOD OF YOUR BUSINESS
- ☞ DEVELOP A SYSTEM OF APPRECIATION
- ☞ NEWSLETTERS
- ☞ DEVELOP AND IMPLEMENT AN EFFECTIVE LEAD GENERATION SYSTEM
- ☞ ENDORSEMENT MARKETING: THE PSYCHOLOGY OF SALES
- ☞ ESTABLISH YOURSELF AS AN EXPERT
- ☞ MAKE IT EASY FOR PEOPLE TO DO BUSINESS WITH YOU
- ☞ STRATEGIC BUSINESS ALLIANCES
- ☞ E-COMMERCE, ON-LINE PROOFING AND WEBPAGES

Develop A Written Marketing Plan

I began this book by asking you ten business practice questions. The first question I asked was whether or not you had a written business/marketing plan. Of all the changes you can make to improve your bottom line, none will have a greater impact than a written business/marketing plan.

IMPACT OF BUSINESS PLAN ON SALES AND INCOME[28]

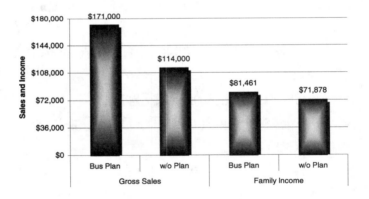

As the above chart illustrates, photographers with written business/marketing plans grossed 50% more than those without written plans. In addition, their family income was over 13% higher.

---

[28] Expanded analysis of the Census 2000, for information on the entire report visit my website at www.marktill.com

The Lucrative Photographer

Why Do Business Plans Have The Impact They Do

The discrepancy in sales and income between studios with and without a written business/marketing plan begs the question, why? I don't believe it is as simple as picking up a piece of paper and jotting down a few ideas. Photographers with written plans have invested a great deal of time to understand their market and their business. They understand their expenses, what they need to charge to pay their bills, and themselves a salary. But more importantly, they have written goals with specific dates for completion. As I noted earlier, putting goals in writing can quadruple your chances of reaching your goals.

Are Business Plans Just For Banks

Formal business plans, complete with market and economic analysis, are primarily designed for companies seeking funding from banks and other financial institutions. Most books on writing business plans are designed with funding in mind.

In the absence of outside funding, small business owners needs are much simpler—a written *marketing plan*. Think of a marketing plan as a road map. It identifies where you are today, where you want to be in a year, two years, five years, etc., and what path you will take to get there. You will still need to create a budget and identify your USP, but the entire plan can be accomplished in a few pages.

To help you get started, below is a list of questions you should ask yourself about where your business is heading. A detailed outline for a business/marketing plan can be found in the appendix.

MARKETING PLAN QUESTIONS[29]

- What products or services will you offer?
- Who will you market to?
- Why should these people do business with you (USP)?
- Can your marketplace support your business?
- How will you get your message to your target audience?
- What are your goals (sittings and sales average) for the next three years?

A WORD OF ENCOURAGEMENT

It is easy to get overwhelmed by this process. Don't worry about creating the perfect marketing plan; there is no such thing. Where many people falter is they never put their plan into action because they never think it is finished. Having a positive attitude and enthusiasm for your business can make up for many shortcomings. Remember, "A marginal plan implemented with passion, most often will outperform an excellent plan implemented marginally".[30]

---

[29] For additional information on products and services to help you create your own written business and marketing plan, visit www.marktill.com or call Mark Till directly at 508-655-9595.
[30] *Selling The Invisible: A Field Guide To Modern Marketing*, Harry Beckwith, ©1997, Warner Books.

What Is The Lifetime Value Of Your Clients?

How much is a client worth to you? Most business professionals have no clue. Often, people look at the immediate sale and fail to see the big picture. To get a sense of what I am talking about, let us look at two clients.

1. Client A makes a one-time purchase of $3,500 and although they were satisfied, you never hear from them again.

2. Client B makes an initial purchase of only $250. However, this client comes back on average two times each year for the next 30 years and makes similar additional purchases. In addition, they refer a few of their friends who also make similar purchases.

Which of these two clients would you prefer to have? To help you decide, below is a worksheet designed to help you calculate the *lifetime value of a single client*. This demonstrates the value of your clients to your business over time. By developing a strong relationship with your clients, you are planting the seeds for future revenue.

In this scenario, the total *lifetime value* to your business from client B is an astounding *510 times his/her initial investment*! In addition client B will generate over

$118,750 more in revenue over the next ten years than client A.

CLIENT LIFETIME VALUE EXAMPLE[31]		
	CLIENT A	CLIENT B
A. Average sale amount	$3,500	$250
B. Sales/Year (buying frequency)	1	2
C. Number of year's Clients buys	1	30
D. Number of referrals from each client	2	10
E. % of referrals that become clients	.75	.75
F. Gross sales per client/year (A*B)	$3,500	$500
G. Gross sales per client (lifetime) (C*F)	$3,500	$15,000
H. Referrals who become clients (D*E)	1.5	7.5
I. Gross sales from referred clients (G*H)	5,250	$111,500
TOTAL LIFETIME VALUE OF A CLIENT (G+I)	$8,750	$127,500

Carl Sewell, in his 1990 book, *Customers For Life: How To Turn That One-Time Buyer Into A Lifetime Customer*, estimated, that the lifetime value of a Cadillac customer (he owns a Cadillac dealership) to be over $332,000! (The average owner buys approximately 12 cars in his or her lifetime, plus the value of maintenance and repairs.) This is over 13 times the original purchase price of $25,000 (the price of a Cadillac at that time). Mr. Sewell doesn't view each transaction as an autonomous occurrence, rather, as part of a long and continuing relationship, and so should you.

As our example shows, the lifetime value of a client goes far beyond the original sale. There are subsequent

<hr>

[31] Examples taken from my monthly on-line survey, to participate visit: http://mark@marktill.com/survey.html

sales, add-on purchases, and referrals! Each time your client refers a new client to you, the cycle begins again and thus multiplies the impact of a client's lifetime value.

This alone should be reason enough for you to want to go out of your way to make your clients love you. However, you can dramatically increase the total lifetime value of a client even further, if you can accomplish three things:

- Increase the transaction dollar amount each client spends.
- Increase the frequency with which clients do business with you.
- Increase the number of clients that you serve. (For example, by increasing the number of referrals.)

The following chart illustrates the sales impact of increasing all three categories from as little as 10% up to 20%.

Status	# of Clients	Average Sale	Buying Frequency	Gross Sales	Growth (%)
THREE WAYS TO GROW YOUR BUSINESS					
Current	100	$250	2	$50,000	N/A
+10 %	110	$275	2.2	$66,550	33%
+12 %	112	$280	2.24	$70,246	40%
+15 %	115	$288	2.3	$76,044	52%
+20 %	120	$300	2.4	$86,400	73%

As you can see, by increasing all three categories (simultaneously) you can increase your sales by as much as 73%!

Let's go back to our lifetime valuation worksheet. If we increased each of the three growth factors just 10%, the lifetime value grows by 33% to $184,676, or more than *twenty-one times* the lifetime value of single purchase client A.

CLIENT LIFETIME VALUE EXAMPLE
EFFECT OF INCREASING ALL THREE FACTORS 10%

		CLIENT A SAME	CLIENT B NEW
A.	Average sale amount	$3,500	$275
B.	Sales/Year (buying frequency)	1	2.2
C.	Number of year's clients buys	1	33
D.	Number of referrals from each client	2	11
E.	% of referrals that become clients	.75	.75
F.	Gross sales per client/year (A*B)	$3,500	$605
G.	Gross sales per client (lifetime) (C*F)	$3,500	$19,965
H.	Referrals who become clients (D*E)	1.5	8.25
I.	Gross sales from referred clients (G*H)	5,250	$164,711
	TOTAL LIFETIME VALUE OF A CLIENT (G+I)	$8,750	$184,676

When you consider that it is five to six times more expensive to attract new business from new clients as compared to attracting new business from existing clients, the message is quite clear—you can make no better investment than doing whatever is necessary to thrill your clients. Yet according to my survey, photographers invest the marketing in the exact opposite direction, spending 77% of their marketing dollars on attracting new business from new clients versus 23% on their existing clients.

The Lucrative Photographer

What is the Life Time Value of your Clients?

Take a few moments to determine your clients' lifetime value. Use the form above as a guide. If you don't know all the answers right now, use your best guest and work on finding the answers in the near future. Once you have estimated your client's lifetime value, think of ways to increase it. Note: The worksheet is based on a single product line, if you offer more than one product, use a different worksheet for each one and total the worksheets together to determine a client's lifetime value.

Client Lifetime Value Worksheet

A.	Average sale amount	$_____
B.	Sales/Year (buying frequency)	$_____
C.	Number of years clients buy	$_____
D.	Number of referrals from each client	$_____
E.	% of referrals that become clients	$_____
F.	Gross sales per client/year (A*B)	$_____
G.	Gross sales per client (lifetime) (C*F)	$_____
H.	Referrals who become clients (D*E)	$_____
I.	Gross sales from referred clients (G*H)	$_____
	Total Lifetime Value of a Client (G+I)	$_____

Spending resources to attract clients that make only a single purchase and are never heard from again (Client A) will not only cost you more to continuously replace your client base, but the clients you replace will spend less. A truly lose—lose situation. Lucrative photographers understand the importance of client retention, which is our next topic.

Marketing and Sales

CROSS-MARKETING POTENTIAL

After your clients' initial purchases, what other
products and services, related to your niche could you
offer to your clients? When I buy a suit the salesperson
always shows me ties, shirts, etc. These extra items can
add up to as much as the suit itself.

This is a very effective marketing strategy. When
people make a purchase, they are more receptive to
suggestions for related products. For instance, when
you go to a restaurant, the waiter will suggest a cocktail
or bottle of wine, an appetizer, and dessert in addition
to the entree. While the entrée pays the bills, the real
profit is in the added extras. What little extras can you
offer your clients? If you photograph weddings, you
can sell an engagement sitting, a signature portrait, a
wall portrait, parent albums, etc. It is important to
remember that the added extras directly relate to the
original product.

Client Retention, The Lifeblood Of Your Business

As I stated earlier, you can make no better marketing investment than with your core clients, those that fit your ideal profile. To illustrate my point, let's look at a few statistics.[32]

THE VALUE OF CLIENT RETENTION

- The top five businesses in any industry have a 93-95% client retention rate, whereas most businesses average 78-82%.
- Most businesses view a loss of a client as a loss of a single transaction rather than the cost of the lifetime value of the client.
- Reducing client defections by as little as 2% per year is the equivalent of cutting costs by 10%!
- For every 1% improvement (sustained over five years) in your client retention rate, there is a 20% improvement in operating income.
- A 5% improvement in your client retention rate can double your profits in five years
- A referral from an existing client will have a 92% retention rate versus a 67% retention rate from a client obtained from advertising.
- A client who comes to you by way of referral is many times more likely to refer other clients to you than a client obtained from traditional advertising methods.

---

[32] Lynn M. Thomas, J.D., President 21st Century Management Consulting

ALL CLIENTS ARE NOT CREATED EQUAL

The best way to gain a new client is through referral and the best way to get referrals is to do everything in your power to keep the clients you have. Well not exactly, you don't want to keep every client, just the ones that are profitable!

However, profitability does not begin with clients, it starts with your target audience. Knowing who your clients are and who they are not can save you a lot of time, money, and effort. The chart above illustrates what is commonly referred to as the *Hierarchy of Clients.*

The chart is in the form of a pyramid for a reason. Each level is built on the foundation of the level before it. The base of the pyramid is the entire universe of *potential* customers for your business. However, not everyone who could use your service will choose to do so. Of those who do become customers some will be more profitable than others. The best of the best is what is referred to as Advocates. It is this elite group of customers that forms the peak of the pyramid. They are the clients who generate 80% of your income and the bulk of your referrals.

HIERARCHY OF CLIENTS

- SUSPECTS—Suspects represent is the entire "universe" of *potential* customers for your business. However, they are not currently aware of you or your company.

- PROSPECTS—Prospects have heard about your company, but have never purchased.

- CUSTOMERS—have purchased one or more times, but not on a regular basis when need exists

- CLIENTS—spend as much as they can with you. You are the first place they go when a relevant need exists

- ADVOCATES—are so satisfied, they continually recommend and endorse you to others - word of mouth promoter of your business

CLIENT CATEGORIES

Another way to view the relative importance of your client base is to divide customers into four categories, A through D.

In categorizing your database, it is helpful to remember the 80/20/80 rule I mentioned earlier. The A clients are the top 20% of your database that generate 80% of your income. Conversely, D clients are the 20% that takes up 80% of your time and actually cost you money to keep.

CLIENT CATEGORY DESCRIPTION

Category	Description
A Advocates (20%)	Generate 80% of your income
B Clients (30%)	Somewhat profitable
C Customers (30%)	Break-even at best
D Hole finders (20%)	Actually cost you money to maintain

The bulk of your clients (60%) fall into either the B or C category. Your B clients are profitable, although probably marginally so, and the C clients spend enough just to cover your costs (break-even).

One of the toughest jobs you face as a business owner is to assess the income potential of the B and C clients. What makes the decision difficult is you probably like these customers and many were instrumental in getting you to where you are today. But in terms of marketing resources you need to make a choice. Your ability to convert B clients into A clients and to weed out the non-profitable C clients will be a contributing factor in determining your long-term success.

Once you have finished assessing the income potential of your customers, it is time to turn your attention to doing everything you can to retain your customers, especially the A clients.

The Lucrative Photographer

CLIENT RETENTION TIPS

We now know what our clients are truly worth, who our best clients are (and are not), and how important it is to keep them happy. The next step is to determine what you can do to increase their loyalty? Below is a list of actions you can take to improve your client retention and increase your number of *Raving Fans (or advocates)*.

Look at things from your clients' perspective—This sounds simple, but you will be surprised to find out how few companies work this way. Everything from the way your studio looks, the way you show your work, the products and services you offer, and even your policies and procedures should be designed with your ideal client in mind. On occasion, there will be a conflict between what is best for your company and what your client wants. The rule of thumb is never to say no to your client; just make the response economically feasible.

This is a lesson I learned the hard way. We don't use paper proofs in our studio and for years we informed prospects and clients that paper previews were no available. We didn't give our clients another option and we quickly realized that our inflexibility was costing us new business. Our solution was not to reverse our policy, but rather we gave our clients the option to have paper proofs; they simply needed to purchase them in order to take them out of our studio. My clients were able to get what they wanted at a price that would make me happy. It is a win-win situation. Remember, try not to say no and remember to look at things from your client's perspective.

Marketing and Sales

You don't create a relationship with clients; you create relationships with human beings, and more specifically, individuals—Try and treat all clients uniquely. Ask them how they would like to be contacted. Some people may prefer to be reached by mail, others by email, phone, etc. If your contact with your client is a positive one you will increase their loyalty by 20%. On the other hand after 2-3 negative contacts, clients are likely to take their business elsewhere.[33]

People don't leave friends—Over the years we have become good friends with many of our clients. In fact I consider this to be one of my greatest accomplishments as a business owner. I am honored that clients treasure our relationship enough to want it to continue beyond its original photographer/client beginnings. Don't simply try to get new clients, look to find new friends.

Increasing client contact decreases client defection—When was the last time you made a purchase and then received a call from the company to find out if everything was all right? How often do you do this with your clients? The number one reason that people switch companies is they feel ignored and under-appreciated (68%). This compares to only 14% who leave because of a bad experience. If someone does leave, find out why. If it is something that can be corrected, do it! When I first started in business, I sent a follow-up letter to people who didn't hire us asking for their feedback. To encourage their response, I told

---

[33] Lynn M. Thomas, J.D., President 21st Century Management Consulting

152

them I would send them a check for $5 just for completing my questionnaire. I usually got a 20-25% response to my survey. The information was invaluable and it helped me identify areas where I needed improvement. On occasion, I would get a call from someone who had a less than happy experience with the photographer they chose. It always pays to be nice.

Hand-written thank you notes, versus typed letters—With modern technology, the hand-written note is almost a lost art. When used properly, a hand-written note can be a powerful marketing tool. The benefits are fairly obvious: people are more likely to open and read a hand-written note versus one generated by computer. Second, hand-written notes are simply more personal.

We use two types of hand-written notes, photo note cards and note pads. I got the idea from reading a book by Bob Burg entitled, *Endless Referrals*. The note cards are 3.5x8 and printed on card stock. The card is designed to fit into a #10 envelope. Information on the card includes my company name, phone and fax number, address, email, web page, and my photograph! The photograph is very important. People buy from people not from companies. The photograph helps people identify me with my company and the products and services I offer. I use the card any time a need arises to send a quick note or other less formal communications. Note-cards cost about the same as business cards and are worth their weight in gold to me.

The note-pad is 5.5x8.5 and is bound 50 sheets to a pad. It fits nicely in the desk size "day-timers type" binder. I include the same information (including my photograph) on the pad plus lines for people to write on. I distribute the pads to clients, reception halls, anyone who needs my services or can refer someone to me who needs my services. People love them. I get calls all the time from people telling me they use my pad all the time and need more.

The pad and note cards help to serve as a constant reminder of who I am and what I offer. People are not going to hire me just because of the pad or the card. However, they are likely to think of me when they need my services and that is what good marketing is all about.

Design specials or products exclusively for your best clients—Most business owners spend too much time worrying about what their competitors are doing when they should be thinking about what *their clients* want and need. Regularly survey your *best (A) clients*. Ask them to tell you what products or services they wished you offered. Many of our most successful products and promotions are a direct result of a conversation I had with a client. Taking care of the needs of your clients is the best way to keep them happy and you one step ahead of the competition.

Handle client complaints quickly and effectively—From time to time you are going to have a client who is less than happy with you and/or your photography. How you handle the situation can mean the difference between a client for life or a public relations nightmare. Research shows that for every $1 you spend in responding *effectively* to client complaints, there is a

$2 benefit to you and your company.[34] Remember, if someone is thrilled with your studio, on average they will tell three people. If they are unhappy or upset, they will complain to ten others. When complaints occur, do what you can (within reason) to resolve the situation quickly. It can be one of the best investments you make.

Be systematic and consistent—Having systems in place to administer programs like these is essential for their success. It is not practical or economical to implement all of these programs at once. Pick one, implement it, refine it, systematize it and move on to the next idea. Once a program is in place, clients will expect to see it over and over again. Consistency breeds familiarity.

HAVING SATISFIED CLIENTS IS NOT GOOD ENOUGH

When was the last time you made a purchase with the expectation that you were going to be disappointed? People make purchases expecting to be satisfied. The same is true for your clients when they hire you. They expect to be treated fairly and for you to make them look good in their photographs. After all, why else would they hire you?

In their book, *Raving Fans*, Ken Blanchard (of *The One-Minute Manager* fame) and Sheldon Bowles explains that to have a lucrative business you need to have people who are willing to sing your praises to whomever they can find. How do you create what they call, *Raving Fans*? You always go the extra mile, which

---

[34] Thomas J. Winninger, *Price Wars: How To Win The Battle For Your Customers*, ©1994 St. Thomas Press

includes customer service, your professional image, and of course, the quality of your photography. It is the sum of the entire package that makes the difference. Your goal is to become indispensable to your clients. If people want you and only you as their photographer, price becomes secondary, client retention improves, and people sing your praises. The result is a *Raving Fan*!

One of the best ways to begin is by looking at what is at stake—which is what is a client really worth to you?

How Do You Handle Predictable Problems?

In spite of our best efforts, we all make mistakes and things do go wrong—we forgot to send in an order, the lab made a mistake, an album arrives damaged, the camera malfunctioned at a critical moment, and the list goes on and on. Problems are part of doing business. Some problems are transparent to the consumer (they never knew there was a problem) others are not. When the latter affects our ability to deliver on our promises to our clients this creates the biggest problem of all—an unhappy client.

Studies have shown that someone who is happy with your services shares their story with three friends. However, if your client is unhappy, they will tell 10 people about their problems. When people are upset they like to tell anyone who will listen. Great customer service comes from how you resolve problems when they occur.

The Lucrative Photographer

Many businesses approach problems on a case-by-case basis, often doing the minimum required to resolve the problem. While this approach may stop your clients' complaints, it may not address a bigger problem, the damage this problem causes to your goodwill. Exceptional customer service seeks not just to fix problems when they occur, but to make the problem-solving process a *memorable, positive experience* your client will want to share.

How often do you hear stories of how a company went above and beyond what was expected to fix a problem. Not often! When you do, it makes a strong statement about how the company values its customers.

How far would you go to make a customer happy? The following story appears in *Knock Your Socks Off Service Recovery*[35].

> *The lobby is deserted. It is not hard to overhear the conversation between the night manager at the Marriott Long Wharf Hotel in Boston and the late arriving guest.*
> *"Yes, Dr. Jones, we've been expecting you. I know you are scheduled to be here three nights. I'm sorry to tell you, sir, but we are booked solid tonight. A large number of guests we assumed were checking out did not. Where is your meeting tomorrow, sir?"*
> *The doctor told the clerk where it was.*

---

[35] *Knock Your Socks Off Service Recovery*, Ron Zemke & Chip R. Bell, ©2000, Amazon Books

"That's near the Omni Parker House! That's not very far from here. Let me call them and get you a room for the evening. I'll be right back."

A few minutes later the desk clerk returned with the good news.

"They're holding a room for you at the Omni Parker House, sir. And, of course, we'll pick up the tab. I'll forward any phone calls that come here for you. Here's a letter that will explain the situation and expedite your check-in, along with my business card so you can call me directly here at the front desk if you have any problems."

The doctor's mood was moving from exasperation toward calm. But the desk clerk was not finished with the encounter. He reached into the cash drawer. "Here are two $5 bills. That should more than cover your cab fare from here to the Parker House and back again in the morning. We don't have a problem tomorrow night, just tonight. And here's a coupon that will get you a complimentary continental breakfast on our concierge level on the fifth floor tomorrow...and again, I am so sorry this happening."

As the doctor walks away, the night manager turns to the desk clerk, "Give him about 15 minutes and then call to make sure everything went okay."

A week later, the same guest who had overheard the exchange is in a taxi, en route to the same hotel. Along the way, he tells of the great service recovery episode he had witnessed the week before. The pair arrived at the hotel and makes their way to the front desk—ready to check in.

The Lucrative Photographer

There they were greeted with the unexpected news.

"I know you were scheduled to be here for two nights. But we are booked solid tonight. Where is your meeting tomorrow?"

The would-be guests exchange a rueful glance as the give the desk clerk their future plans.

"That's near the Meridien Hotel. Let me call over there and see if I can get you a room. It won't take but a minute."

As the clerk walks away, the taleteller says. "I'll bet he comes back with a letter and a business card."

Sure enough, the desk clerk returns to deliver the solution; not a robotic script, but all the elements from the previous week's show were on display. The taleteller thought what he had witnessed the previous week was pure desk clerk initiative. He now realizes the desk clerk's actions were planned; a spontaneous-feeling yet predetermined response to a specific category of customer problem.

The point at which your customer is most insecure is where your organization's front line should be most confident. In other words, at that juncture where your customer is most insecure because things are not turning out as anticipated, your front line should be best equipped to ease the anxiety. Planned recovery arms front-line service people with the confidence and competence to turn distress into delight.

The Marriott did not have to pick up the tab for the hotel, pay for the taxi, or provide a complimentary breakfast. However, by doing so, they turned an otherwise disgruntled customer into a loyal client.

Take a look at the top three to five *predictable problems* you know will occur in your studio. How have you handled these problems in the past? Using the Marriott example, look for ways you can turn these problems into a positive experience for your clients. The gestures don't have to be grand in scale—offer to pay for shipping, provide a folio with a few of their favorite images, and use your imagination. It is also an excellent idea to get your clients involved in the process. More often than not, clients will ask for less than you are willing to offer. (But don't forget to give them a little extra for the inconvenience.)

When you consider the cost of acquiring a new client and the potential lifetime value to your studio, going the extra mile to make the client happy is not only a good policy, it is a great *long-term* investment as well.

Develop A System Of Appreciation

According to the *Thank-You Institute,* the second week in January is National "thank your customer" week. The idea is based on the Japanese practice of **Ningen Kankei** (Human Relations), in which they take the time each year to show their customers how much they value their patronage. Feeling under appreciated, *not* product dissatisfaction is the number one reason customers leave and use a different company. Remarkably, only 10% of photographers have a formal system for customer appreciation.

THE IMPORTANCE OF SAYING THANK-YOU

You just purchased a custom-made product. Although it cost a lot more than you planned for, you rationalize the purchase, in part based on the connection or friendship with the salesperson. After delivery, overall you are pleased with the result. However, you do not receive a call to make sure you are pleased with the product or to thank you for your purchase.

A few weeks later you make a purchase of an item that costs less than $30. Two days after your purchase you receive a call from the company thanking you for your patronage and to make sure everything was okay with the product they sold you.

While the above examples are fictitious, the former could be photography and the latter a service like having the oil changed in your car. Customer appreciation is not dependent on the amount of money a customer spends. When was the last time you received a call after the purchase to make sure everything was okay? It's easy to remember because it doesn't happen very often, but when it does, how does it make you feel?

As part of the Census 2000, I asked photographers to rank the reasons they believe customers hire them. Customer service was listed fourth. Yet, nearly 6 out of 10 photographers fail to follow-up with customers after delivery.[36] Another 3 out of 10 do so only occasionally.

After Sales Follow-up

always 13%

never 57%

sometimes 30%

People who are either really upset or really happy will say something. (This is especially true if they are really upset.) However, the majority of people will not complain *even if they are unhappy* because they don't believe anyone wants to know what they think. If something is not exactly what they wanted and you don't follow-up, the problem just lingers and the next time a need for your services arises, they go somewhere else.

---

[36] Census 2000, Mark Till Consulting, Professional Photographers of America

DISTINGUISH YOURSELF BY SHOWING YOU CARE

The number one reason (67%) why customers switch from one company to another is because they didn't feel the former appreciated their business. Based on the above statistics, it is easy to see why. Great customer service is not limited to what you do *before* the sale; it is also how you show your appreciation *after* the sale.

If you are looking for a way to give yourself a competitive advantage over your competition, start by saying thank-you.

THINK STRATEGICALLY

By now it should come as no surprise that I recommend developing a formal system to show customer (and employee) appreciation. What do you want to accomplish by implementing a system of appreciation? Will you have different levels of gift giving?

It is always a good idea to establish goals whenever you begin a new project. Otherwise, how will you measure its success? Keep in mind, gifts and thank-you notes are just like advertising, you need to be committed to the process for a long enough period for you to see any results. Most people give up on marketing before it has a chance to succeed.

Consider having different levels of gift giving. For example you may simply want to send a thank-you note for a referral but a gift basket for a new client. Also think about those individuals who send you multiple new clients each year. Instead of giving the same gift over and over, consider doing something unique and different, such as a donation to their favorite charity in their name.

Develop A System Consistent With Your Marketing Efforts And Studio Image

The quality of gifts should reflect the quality of your work, studio image, and quality your clients would expect for themselves. I can't stress this enough. A gift that looks cheap and inexpensive is worse than sending no gift at all.

Try to keep in mind items and gifts that tie back to your business. For example I send our wedding clients watercolor note-cards printed with one of their favorite images as a thank-you gift while their album order is being processed. I have also sent a framed desk size portrait to my top clients on their first anniversary. (It is the paper anniversary.) Other examples include a gift basket with a silver frame, or a jewelry box with a photograph on top. All these gifts work because there is a logical connection to our core business.

One of the best client appreciation ideas I have come across is from fellow photographer, Angela Carson. Each year she has a huge client appreciation picnic complete with pony rides and face painting. I have heard Angela tell stories from past years and it makes me want to be a client just so I can attend!

REASONS TO SEND CARDS

Notes and cards are a great way to increase contact with your clients. Some of the more traditional occasions include:

* Thank you
* New job
* Holidays

* Birthdays
* Anniversaries
* Moving

Don't limit yourself to the traditional holidays such as Christmas and Valentine's Day. Why not send a card for Halloween or Ground Hog's Day. Sending cards and gifts on "off" holidays will get you more attention.

DON'T FORGET YOUR EMPLOYEES

Money only motivates people for a short period of time. Remember that it's your employees who make you look good every day of the week. It could be something as simple as tickets to a movie, a gift certificate for dinner, or a weekend getaway. The most outrageous thank-you I have ever seen was from a local furniture store. They closed all their stores one Monday and took every employee to Bermuda for the day. They also took some local reporters to document the event for the news that evening. Now that's a thank-you! (And good publicity!)

It is vital to have systems in place to make the process work and to be done consistently. To be truly effective, the process has to be simple and almost automatic. A good ad specialty company can be an invaluable asset. The company I use has helped me systematize and simplify the entire process. For example, I ordered coffee mugs with our corporate logo, they store the mugs in their warehouse and whenever I need to send one to a client, I call/fax in the necessary information. The company then fills the mug with different types of treats and ships it out for me. The company also keeps track of which gifts I sent and to whom, so I don't send the same gift twice.

When you stop to consider the lifetime value of your customers, gifts and thank you notes is a small investment to make to improve client loyalty.

Newsletters

Personally I think newsletters are one of the most cost-effective marketing tools available to small business owners, yet only 20% of photographers responding to my survey have a studio newsletter. This section outlines the benefits of having a newsletter and tips on how to get started.

BENEFITS

Establishes you as an expert—People prefer to do business with a specialist, someone who is an expert in his or her field. A newsletter provides you with a forum to showcase your talents and knowledge of photography. The objective is simple, when people think of your style (niche) of photography, you are the first and only name that comes to mind.

Identify and solve client problems—One of the best ways to make yourself an invaluable resource to your clients is to offer solutions to the key concerns, issues, and problems facing your clients. People relate better to stories of people who have faced similar experiences to their own. If you can demonstrate how you helped another client solve a particular problem, people reading your newsletter will assume you can do the same for them. Make a connection to your clients' heart, and they'll reward your wallet.

Educate clients and prospects—Do people know what to wear to a sitting? Do they know when the best times are to photograph their children? How about choosing the best size for a wall portrait or designing the ideal wedding album? The auto industry has convinced us we need to change our oil every 3,000 miles, dentists have made teeth cleaning every six months a standard, and who do you think convinced brides and grooms about how much to spend on their engagement ring? Would you rather educate your clients or would you prefer they get the answer from their friends who shop at the mass-market studios for portraits and frames? Be proactive; educate through your newsletter.

Introduce new products—You've just come back from a seminar or convention and you got an idea or two for a new product (consistent with your niche, of course) and you can't wait to introduce it to your clients. A newsletter is a terrific medium. You can show a photograph, describe the benefits, get a few testimonials from happy clients, and possibly offer an incentive. The trick is to make the article less a sales piece and more information/news in tone. A newsletter will quickly lose its appeal if it becomes simply a four page sales letter. By making the newsletter informative, you will have people looking forward to getting it. Sales will come, be patient.

Cross-market other services—One thing I learned from selling insurance and investments was that my clients tended to identify me with the first product or service I sold them. If I sold them life insurance, they were surprised I sold investments, etc. My point is that many of your clients are probably unaware of many of the products and services you offer simply because they either didn't need them at the time, or they were unaware you offered them at all. The newsletter is your opportunity to convert a one-time purchase into a lifetime client.

Preempt competition—One of the tried and true axioms of marketing is, it is better to be first than it is to be the best (being both is even better). If you are the first studio to be fully digital or offer prints on the Internet, brag about it in your newsletter. If the public hears about it from you first, you will always be associated with it. Always maximize a publicity opportunity.

Win back past clients—By sending a newsletter out on a consistent basis, you can reclaim orphaned clients, people who you haven't done business with for a long while. I am always pleasantly surprised when I get a phone call from a client I have not spoken with in several years. They always tell me how much they enjoy receiving the newsletter, and because of my persistence, they have thought of me, now that they have the need for my services again.

GETTING STARTED

Now that you've decided to offer a newsletter, what is involved? No surprise the first step is planning:

Establish goals—What do you want to accomplish with your newsletter? Is your primary purpose to increase business, or maybe it's to encourage more referrals, or is it simply to create goodwill. Whatever your goal is, write it down and decide how you will measure its success. A quality newsletter takes time and money. Establishing goals and objectives can help you determine if a newsletter is worth the effort.

Marketing and Sales

Who is your target audience—As with your niche, knowing who your audience is and is not is vital to the long-term success of your newsletter. A newsletter targeted to professionals needing publicity photos will have a totally different look and feel from a newsletter aimed at high school seniors. If you do have more than one target audience, (and I don't recommend you do) consider separate newsletters for each audience aimed at its specific needs. (As we'll see in the next section, the quality of your mailing list is a major factor in the success of any marketing effort.)

Research clients' needs and interests—Once you know what your goals are and whom you want to send your newsletter to, the next step is to determine what to write about. The content of your newsletter should be developed with the clients' needs in mind.

Develop a budget—Even if you create and publish your newsletter internally, the cost can get out of hand if you don't establish a budget first. Newsletters do take time to organize and produce. Consistency is very important. You are better off starting out with a small simple newsletter distributed on a regular basis than a more elaborate one that comes out as time and money permits.

Title and subtitle—How often have you seen a good but not spectacular print score well in competition because it had a great name and presentation? Your newsletter is no different. The name should be consistent with your niche and tell the reader why they should take the time to read your newsletter.

The banner (logo)—It is vitally important that your logo and look of your newsletter be consistent with the rest of your collateral material. A newsletter that looks cheap will make you look the same. Be very protective of your studio image. Also, don't forget *your* photograph. You are the reason people hire your studio. Placing your photograph on your newsletter (and all collateral material) helps identify you with your studio and your niche.

Distribution—Until recently, the only real option was printing and mailing a newsletter. Today with the Internet, it is practical to have your newsletter on your webpage or sent to prospects and clients via email. Determine which method or combination of methods your target audience prefers. Your objective is to determine the best way to get this information into your clients' hands and have them read it.

CONTENT AND DESIGN ELEMENTS

These are basic elements that all successful newsletters should contain. They include:

- *Primary article*—Main/feature story, the title should state an important problem, issue, or concern you know your readers have.
- *Secondary article*—Is typically shorter in length and should be consistent with your main article theme.
- *Illustrations*—If properly done, illustrations and photographs will break up your text into appealing portions and bolster your story.

- *Typography*—To avoid the plain vanilla look, consider using drop caps, tinted screens, and callout boxes.
- *White space*—Remember to allow a little breathing room when designing your page layout. It is easier for people to read.
- *Call to action*—Don't forget to ask your readers to respond in some fashion. You may want your reader to respond to a special offer or simply to call to request more information.

REMIND THEM WHY THEY CHERISH PHOTOGRAPHS

Newsletters can enhance your relationship with your clients, create a strong emotional connection, and offer solutions to their problems. Give your clients a reason to not only look forward to receiving the newsletter, but participating in it as well. One of the powerful ways to do so is with stories.

An excellent example of this was an article I read in the *Boston Globe* in 1997 by Renee Loth entitled: *Why Do We Cherish Photographic Memories?* Ms. Loth was reminiscing about a photograph she found while cleaning her mother's attic. She asked, "Why does this picture move me so?" Her response is something all of us, as photographers, should take to heart...

"...Perhaps it (the photograph) contains such promise—all the DNA of the future is right there—but it also captures a moment in time that is so ephemeral.

The Lucrative Photographer

...The picture like all spurs to the memory tells us something about our relationship to time. The reason we connect so viscerally to our past is that we carry it with us always, just as the present moment will be found in our futures. Anyone who has done any exploration of relationships knows that we are inexorably shaped by our histories. But my reaction to the picture proves that the past is not a dead thing, fixed and remote. It is always accessible, albeit concealed under layers of current experience. It takes only a signal, like a ringing bell that resonates through time, and an open heart, to remember."

I wanted to share this story because it is easy to forget what our images mean to our customers. Think about all the film that is sold to consumers. The number of digital cameras they use to email their photos to loved ones around the globe. Why people enjoy watching home movies so much. It is because of the connection to the past, present, and future that Ms. Loth so eloquently described.

A DIFFICULT TIME TO BE THANKFUL

People use lots of excuses to put off having a family portrait. However, the tragic events of September 11, 2001 remind us that there is no time like the present to have our families photographed.

An article in the *Boston Globe* which appeared shortly after the tragedy, interviewed several people who lost loved ones in the attack. A woman whose husband was one of the victims said, "she is grateful that just weeks before…they'd arranged to have a professional family photograph taken". Imagine how this family would have felt if they postponed the portrait sitting?

Contact your customers and have them relate their stories to you. Have a contest on how they met, or what their children mean to them. A newsletter is a wonderful medium to share these memories along with your images and to remind clients why they cherish photographs.

Develop And Implement
An Effective Lead Generation System

Marketing expert Bob Martel, of JMB Marketing, believes the key to marketing success is having and implementing an effective *lead generation system*. Lead generation is what marketing is all about and having an effective system helps ensure that your marketing efforts get implemented. Yet far too often the only marketing photographers use is paid advertising. Magazine companies, bridal shows, and the yellow pages all have a sales force that regularly solicit photographers to advertise in their publications. Fearing that if they don't advertise, they won't be able to survive, photographers place ads and sit back waiting for their phones to ring.

Unfortunately, successful marketing is not a passive activity. To be truly lucrative, you need to be proactive in your marketing efforts. The good news is that lead generation systems often cost a lot less than print advertising. Examples of lead generation systems include direct response marketing, networking, and referrals.

DIRECT RESPONSE MARKETING

Direct response marketing includes sales letters, postcards, and ads that are aimed at a targeted group of people with the intent of having them call to purchase your product/service or request additional information.

Marketing and Sales

Many business owners use a *one-step approach* to their direct response marketing in which the mailing comes right out and asks for the prospect's business. This works well with your existing clients, since they already know you. For the mailing to be successful, you simply need an attractive offer.

If you are completely unknown to the prospect, and you are offering a high-ticket item, a *two-step approach* may be more effective. The objective here is not to generate an immediate sale, but rather to compile a list of qualified prospects. The offer may include a free report or information kit. Once the prospect takes his or her initial action, you contact them to convert them into clients. This approach requires a little more patience, but in the long run, it can generate a highly targeted mailing list full of qualified prospects.

Regardless of which technique you use, you need to remember the *40-40-20 rule*. Forty percent of the success of a direct marketing piece is mailing it to the right people. As I have said over and over again, you need to know who your target audience is. Nowhere is it more important than when you use direct marketing. A great letter and great offer that is sent to the wrong group would not generate any new business. Another 40% of the success is who you are and what you are offering. People have to want or need what you have to sell. As the saying goes, "Make them an offer they can't refuse." Finally, only 20% of the success of a direct mail campaign is the format and what you say. A great offer and a highly targeted list mailed out on photocopy paper are better than a fancy brochure without an offer mailed indiscriminately.

The Lucrative Photographer

Have you ever noticed that successful people seem to know everyone? This is no accident. The top performers in any profession are avid networkers.

There are different types of networking organizations. The first type is what I refer to as lead generation groups. One of the largest examples of this type of group is Business Network International (BNI). In a lead generation group, people get together on a regular basis (usually weekly) for the sole purpose of exchanging leads. Typically, membership is limited to one person per category. For example, there would be only one photographer per group. It is important for you to choose a group whose members are marketing to your target audience. If not, you may end up with lots of leads from the wrong type of prospect.

The next category is a casual or generic networking group. The Chamber of Commerce is a good example. Chambers often host networking breakfasts and business after hours events where you can meet other members and develop business relationships. I have made lots of friends and valuable contacts through my association with my local Chamber that goes beyond networking. The goal of networking should not simply be to generate more business (although it will happen). Many of the vendors I use, I originally met through networking. Networking is a valuable resource; use it to its fullest.

Third is an industry specific group. As a wedding photographer, it is important for me to network with the catering sales people in the hotels in my area.

Consequently, I belong to a group called *The National Associations of Catering Executives* (N.A.C.E.). My local chapter meets once each month, and I have become friends with people in a position to refer their clients to me. Over the years it has been consistently my top lead generation source.

Finally, the fourth category is civic-minded organizations such as Rotary, Lions Club, church groups, and non-profits (March of Dimes, American Cancer Society, etc.). The purpose of these organizations is to benefit the community as a whole. You participate because you want to help others. Although getting business is not the reason I join these organizations, I can tell you I have made some wonderful contacts and gotten more than a few photography jobs as an added bonus.

Networking should not be limited to any one-type of organization. Ideally you should belong to one in each category. A word of caution: It is easy to get caught up in going to meeting after meeting, after meeting. Be strategic. You can't possibly attend every group available. Keep your business (and personal) objectives in mind. It is better to be very active in a few groups than it is to be a casual participant in many.

ASK FOR REFERRALS

Getting referrals is natural part of business. If you provide a quality product or service, eventually word gets around regardless of whether you intentionally try to promote referrals or not. However, if you want to get most of your business through word of mouth, you're going to have to help the process along.

The Lucrative Photographer

Who doesn't want to get more business through referral? Referred prospects are easier to close, have fewer complaints, are more loyal, and remain clients longer.[37] Best of all, referrals cost little to no money to obtain. So why aren't photographers more aggressive in seeking referrals? No one taught them how and again, to be successful, it requires them to make a proactive effort.

I have to admit, I don't ask for referrals as often as I should. Anytime you have contact with your clients is a good time to ask for referrals. This process should begin with your first appointment. When someone asks me how much I charge, I tell them we get compensated in three ways. First, there is a fee for our time to be at your wedding. Second, there is a minimum purchase required. And third, if you are happy with the work and service we provide you, we will want you to refer us to your friends and relatives who could benefit from our services as well. Clients are put on notice right from the beginning that we will be asking for referrals from time to time.

Many years ago I wanted to find a way to encourage clients to refer more business to me. The idea I came up with was a Dinner/Referral Program. In a nutshell, for every referral that became a client, we bought the referring client dinner and once a quarter their name was entered into a drawing for a weekend getaway. We published the names of the clients who made the referral as well as the grand prizewinner in our

---

[37] *Business by Referral, A Sure-Fire Way to Generate New Business*, Ivan Misner, Ph.D. & Robert Davis, ©1998 Bard Press.

newsletter. It didn't take long before the number of referrals picked up. Keep in mind, promotions like this will work only if you do a good job for your clients and they are happy with your services. If you still need a reason to ask for more referrals, remember that people who come to you by referral are more likely to refer someone else to you than someone who heard about you through traditional advertising.

THE KEY IS BEING PROACTIVE

All lead generation's methods require taking a proactive role. Many business owners shy away from proactive marketing because of fear of rejection. It is easier and safer to place an ad and hope the phone will ring. Let's face it, if marketing was easy, we would all be wealthy. If you're uncomfortable in sales, either learn to like it, or hire someone who does. Implementing an effective lead generation system is the difference between just surviving and being lucrative.

Endorsement Marketing

Trust is the assured reliance on the character, ability, strength, or truth of someone or something[38]

Have you ever purchased a camera, lens, flash, background, prop, filter, etc. because a well-known photographer or speaker said they use one of those products themselves? If so, you know first hand the power of *endorsement marketing.*

When used properly, *endorsement marketing* can be one of the most powerful and effective marketing tools available to you because it draws on the trust and goodwill we place on those we know. Think of your own experience. If you made a purchase based on someone's recommendation, it is likely you did so because you viewed that person as a credible source.

WHY PEOPLE BUY

Goodwill is the favor or prestige that a business has acquired beyond the mere value of what it sells[39]

Endorsement marketing is effective because it is based on how we make purchasing decisions. If you understand the human factors involved in making purchasing decisions, you can use them to influence prospects to use your services. There are four key human factors to consider in any marketing strategy:

---

[38] Webster's Dictionary
[39] Webster's Dictionary

Marketing and Sales

- *Emotion, not logic*—How will your customer feel as a result of using your services. Why do you think car dealers want you to "test" drive a car? To experience ownership. Look for ways to engage prospects on an emotional level. Why are they having the images created, how will they be displaying the finished prints, what do their children mean to them, etc.?

- *A preponderance of "social proof"*—This factor is based on the principal that if enough people say the product is good, it must be so. "Four out of five doctors recommend...." What can you do to convince your prospect, with absolute certainty you can do all that you promise? One of the best methods is the use of testimonials. Remember why you bought that lens filter? Testimonials.

- *Fear, greed, and scarcity*—The less available something is, the more valuable it becomes. People want what they can't have. Suppose you only have one evening appointment per week. A prospect calls to see you but you inform him/her it will take 3-4 weeks to get an evening appointment. Instead of risking that you will be unavailable on their date, they make an appointment to see you during the day that week.

- *The law of reciprocity*—I like to refer to this as good old-fashioned guilt. If someone has done you a favor, it is only natural for you to want to reciprocate in kind.

The Lucrative Photographer

Endorsement Marketing Techniques

Whatever your business situation is or product or service you offer, the method is essentially the same. Begin by looking for a person to endorse your studio. Think of someone you worked with recently who was thrilled with your work and fits your profile for the ideal client. Approach this person and ask if they would mind sending a letter of endorsement (on their letterhead) to colleagues, family, friends, etc., telling them about you and what you did for them. The quality, not quantity of their list is critical. The person who is endorsing you needs to be in a position of influence or have a high degree of credibility with the person the letter will be sent to.

The letter should contain a testimonial from the sender and an offer from you via the sender. For example, *"I have asked Mark, as a special favor to me, if he would...."* Remember to incorporate the four human factors in why people buy into your letter.

You would then send a follow-up letter (to the list of prior recipients) a week or two later thanking the endorser for the kind words and restating the offer. You may even want to send a third letter or follow-up with a personal phone call.

What's In It For The Endorser?

I am often asked, "Why would someone want to endorse you?

- First, you did an exceptional job for them!
- You did them a favor (guilt).

- They want to use your services as gifts to their friends, colleagues, employees, customers, etc.
- It creates goodwill, and
- They are being compensated to do so. (A flat fee, a commission based on sales, or a simple gift).

Of course not everyone will want to send out an endorsement letter. However, if you have established goodwill with your clients, they will be more than happy to help you out.

People who come to you by means of referral are more loyal as clients and are more likely to refer additional clients to you than their counterparts.

One of the reasons I like endorsement marketing is it is easy to use, it doesn't require a lot of cash to implement, and it works equally as well regardless if you just started out or are well established. To learn more about endorsement marketing and how it can work for you, visit www.marktill.com/jmbem/html.

The Lucrative Photographer

Establish Yourself As An Expert

WRITE AN ARTICLE OR COLUMN IN A LOCAL PAPER
Considering the potential free publicity (and prestige) writing an article or column in a local paper can bring. I am always amazed at how few photographers take advantage of this golden opportunity. Writing an article in your local paper can be even more valuable than publicity because you are controlling the content. Many local papers have limited staffing and can be receptive to having someone submit an article or periodic column. The key is the article *or column has to be of value to their readers* and not an ad for your services in disguise.

The benefits are often long lasting. For example, one day I was at a restaurant with a colleague when someone came by to say hello to her husband. The gentlemen commented on how much he has enjoyed reading my colleague's column in the local paper. After he left she confided in me that she had not written for that paper in over a year.

When I mention writing an article, people usually ask, "What should I write about?" Use your imagination. If you photograph children you could write about how parents can take better snap shots. The column could be on photography in general—how to take great fireworks photographs on the Fourth of July, vacation photograph tips, etc. The point is you are an expert in your field. By writing an article or column you *increase your visibility* and solidify your position and prestige in your community.

Marketing and Sales

PUBLIC SPEAKING

Writing a column can also make you a sought after speaker for church and temple groups, Rotary Clubs, etc. When papers and television stations do feature stories on photography, whom do you think they will call to interview? How much did all this publicity cost you? Not one cent! (In fact some places will pay you to speak.) How much do you think it would cost in print ads to reach the same number of people?

As with any marketing effort, it is important to keep your target audience in mind. Accordingly, the publications you write for and the places you speak at should be aimed at your ideal clients. For instance, if you photograph children, the local parent paper is a good choice. Make publishing articles or writing a column part of your overall marketing strategy—you'll be amazed by the results.

PUBLICITY

Simply stated, publicity consists of stories about you and your company that appear in any type of media, such as newspapers, radio, magazines, TV, etc. The good news is publicity is almost always free, it helps establish you as an expert, and it improves your creditably in the marketplace. The bad news (if there is any) is you have no control over when stories get published, how they are presented, or when they are run. However, on the whole, publicity can be a tremendous boost to your business if you use it effectively.

The Lucrative Photographer

How often have you heard about a particular product or service in the news and subsequently went out and purchased it? This is the power of publicity, and it is one of the fastest ways you can use to make a name for yourself. For example, look at Ebay. When they first got started there was a lot of press around the new concept of an on-line auction house. As a result, their business took off. Sure, others have copied them, but Ebay has successfully associated their name with their industry.

The same is true for many of the top brands (or in our case, studios) in each industry. Lucrative businesses use a combination of publicity and advertising to make their business name a household word with their target audience. In their book, *The Twenty-Two Immutable Laws Of Branding: How To Build A Product Or Service Into A World-Class Brand,* Al and Laura Ries go even further. They believe brand names are *created* through publicity, not advertising. While advertising keeps your name in the minds of the buying public, it is publicity that gives your company's name the initial name recognition it needs.

I am a big believer is submitting press releases for everything I do, and I send them out as often as I can with very good results. When I first began selling images over the Internet with E-Prints, I sent press releases everywhere. The local papers printed the articles verbatim, which was nice, but it also caught the attention of the larger papers including *The Boston Globe,* they did a feature article on some of our clients and us. My crowning jewel (to date) was being interviewed by the *Wall Street Journal,* complete with a photograph of my studio.

While being published is great for one's ego, the bottom line is, does it generate any business? Absolutely! Several years ago, I wrote a press release about designing albums on the computer and all the fun things related to the technology. I got a phone call from a bride who read the article. Her photographer had given her all the negatives and proofs from the wedding. She was unhappy with a few images and asked if I could help her. We ended up "swapping heads" on a few images and she was so pleased she ordered an album for herself, her mother, and mother-in-law for a total order of over $3,500!

So how does one get started? I asked my friend Abe Dane, who spent many years as a journalist to share some of his thoughts and advice on the subject. Abe recommends the following to anyone wishing to get a press release published:

- Identify publications you want to get press in.
- Learn what they are about; identify the names of the columnists who write about the things you do.
- Look for the spots in the paper where you want to be.
- Know the by-lines of the different reporters to know what each wants to hear.
- Identify each publication formula (style). The same topics appear in the same place on a regular basis.

- Local publications (usually weekly) like it if you make their job easier—that is, send a press release in a format that is ready to go to press.
- Make sure the story goes to the right person. Abe's wife, Jan, had grown tired of all the negative articles on pit bulls and wrote a response to the paper. She had sent it to the editorial section where it got no response. Subsequently, she noticed a column by a person who liked to write about topics that are related to her story, and she sent her letter to him. Within a few days the writer contacted her, and a story about her and their dog appeared in the paper.
- It is better to submit articles using your own letterhead. It makes it more personal.
- There is a difference between the small locals and the larger publications. The smaller publications will want you to help write the article, the larger publications will want to interview you and write the piece themselves. Your press release should reflect the different styles.
- Sending a photograph and all necessary camera-ready artwork is a big help. Make their lives easier.
- Being a good photographer is NOT newsworthy.

Any marketing expert will tell you that the first step in marketing a product or service is to make your target audience aware of its existence. Publicity is one of the fastest and least expensive ways to quickly get your message out. Make a regular habit of sending out press releases to the publications that are read by your clients. Don't forget local television, you never know when they might do a story on photography. The first person they want to contact should be you.

SEMINARS AND WORKSHOPS

Studies have shown that people will pay more for advice than they will for a product. One of the ways to encourage your clients to call you with questions is to conduct seminars. With the possible exception of writing an article or column, seminars and workshops may be the most underutilized marketing resource available to photographers. When was the last time you heard about a photographer sponsoring a seminar for his or her clients? Probably never. Have you or someone you know purchased a book or other product from the person or company presenting at a seminar?

Seminars are successful for several reasons. First, they provide you with a qualified list of potential buyers. People attend seminars because they want or need what the presenter is offering. Otherwise, why else would they attend? Second, it is a way of rewarding your existing client base by offering a value-added service. Third, it increases your presence in the marketplace. Whether people attend or not, your name gets circulated among your target audience. And finally, seminars can cost next to nothing to put on, particularly if you partner with other businesses that want to market to the same people.

Anytime you have an opportunity to be in front of your target audience or have them visit your studio, do it. It will solidify your relationship and ultimately increase buying frequency, a key element in the lifetime value of clients.

Make It Easy For People To Do Business With You

ENCOURAGE SALES WITH A ROCK-SOLID GUARANTEE.

One of the best ways to encourage a prospect to move forward with the sale is to have a rock-solid guarantee. I am sure each and every one of us has at one time or another made a purchase because the salesperson or company said, "If you don't like it, you can return it for a full refund." What did you have to lose? This is the point of a guarantee; as a client, you risk nothing.

Don't be afraid to honor it. People who worry are those who don't do good work and would never dream of providing a guarantee. Most photographers I know would gladly re-shoot a portrait session or re-print a photograph to make a client happy. Since you are already, in effect, guaranteeing your work anyway, why not get credit for it.

Keep in mind, the guarantee has to be genuine with little or no strings attached, otherwise people won't take it seriously. While a guarantee does not work in every situation, I encourage you to use it whenever you can. If you produce quality work you will rarely have to put the guarantee into place.

USE TESTIMONIALS TO SPREAD YOUR GOOD NAME

Testimonials add credibility to your company. People want to feel good about their purchase. Reading about how other people have benefited from your services makes prospects more willing to purchase from you.

191

Isn't a referral a form of a testimonial? Yet, how often have you seen client testimonials on someone's website, brochure, print ad, price list, etc.? Not as often as you would expect.

Use client testimonials as often as you can. Remember, you do need to get their permission if you intend to use them on the web or in other publications. *Don't ever make them up;* it will only undermine your credibility. Include as much information as the source will allow (name, city, title, and company). Look for testimonials that reflect your niche and image.

Strategic Business Alliances

Strategic business alliances are vendors working together to reach the same clients. For example, as a wedding photographer, you might work with a videographer, florist, caterer, band, etc. to attract the same bride.

Strategic alliances are not new. How many of you use a particular credit card because you get airline miles? I switched so Laura and I could fly to Hawaii in First Class. Movie studios and toy companies have for years had strategic alliances, creating action figures of the movie characters.

Alliances can be short-term in nature or ongoing. For the alliance to succeed, there needs to be mutual benefit and trust. Look for vendors you would want to do business with. After all, by forming an alliance you are endorsing their product or service. As with any partnership, you should also have an exit strategy in case the alliance does not work out.

Earlier we discussed seminars. If your studio is too small to conduct a seminar, consider doing one with another vendor. A client of mine did just that by having a children's fashion show. She made an arrangement with a local children's clothing store, along with a caterer and a florist and used her clients' children as the models. It was a big success! She was able to showcase her work, get her clients involved in a fun activity, and made valuable relationships with other vendors who serve the same clients.

My same client hosted an open house with all the vendors located in the same shopping mall. There was food, balloons, clowns, etc. Do you think she has made herself a valuable resource to her clients? You bet, and the next time they need a portrait, whom do you think they will call?

E-Commerce Strategies

"Asking how the Internet will affect photography is like asking how television affected the film industry," says Abe Dane, co-founder of *E-Prints*, one of the first companies to offer on-line sales of photography. He continued by saying, "The Internet has grown faster than television ever did. It gives photographers a new way to show and distribute their work and will have a tremendous impact on the way studios will conduct themselves in the future."

Abe is not alone. John St-Pierre, President of *PhotosAtMyDoor*, claims that the online environment for photographers has changed drastically in the last couple of years: "When the first phase of photographers came online most of them did so for clients to get information about their studio, when the second phase of photographers came online they did so to post and sell images online, now the third phase has arrived where photographers can not only have a website with information but they can also post and sell images, conduct e-commerce and conduct marketing programs with e-marketing," says John.

Ken Wilson, owner of *LustreColor lab* in Canton, Massachusetts, believes that few products have ever been introduced that will have a greater impact on the income of photographers as the Internet and related e-commerce (the sale of goods and services over the Internet).

PICTURES ARE AT THE CORE OF
WHAT HAS MADE THE INTERNET SUCCESSFUL

The Internet combines the ability to exchange information and images with peoples' desire to share their memories with friends and loved ones, making it a perfect fit for photographs. People who may not have had access to your images before can now share the memories and thus multiply your ability to sell images to a wider audience. As an industry, we are just beginning to take advantage of what the web has to offer and opportunity for growth is abundant.

According to recent industry estimates, the number of new users to the web is growing at an astounding rate of 55% per year. More amazingly, the annual growth rate of e-commerce, the sale of goods and services over the Internet, is a staggering 155%. When you consider that fact, having an on-line strategy is now a necessity.

The reality is that 6 out of 10 of your customers and/or potential customers are online today and the numbers are just going to continue to grow. The public already gets their photographs digitized from the local labs and for less than $49 can use software that will create slide shows, add music, and send images across the web. "If consumers can get this type of digitized images from one-hour labs, it makes sense for professional photographers to offer digital proofing as well," notes Ken Wilson

Gene Gessert from *UpdateSoftware*, a company that specializes in software and services to allow business owners to build and maintain their own website, has a slightly different perspective.

The Lucrative Photographer

"Photography presents an interesting case in that selling photographic prints on a website suffers from none of the disadvantages of e-commerce. In fact it is one of the rare cases where the product could, in theory, be delivered on line. On the other hand, photography as it is traditionally practiced, exploits few of the Internets advantages," according to Gene.

Photographers need to learn how to take advantage of the Internet's potential for low cost customer communication and an automated customer interface (to view and purchase images).

A Tool For Perspective Clients To View And Evaluate A Photographer

Just like a visit to your studio, you want your clientele to see immediately what separates you from the other photographers they visited on the Web before and after you. It is reasonable to assume that potential clients searching for a photographer online click from site to site trying to find the perfect match or photographer with the most impressive work. Your website must be not only professional, but also a reflection of you and your business.

Technology now allows photographers to update and change their own sites when desired. This provides you with the ability to edit and change images on your webpage as soon as new ones become available. Before posting or when re-evaluating your website consider asking several clients, friends, family, or colleagues to visit your site and ask them for the first 5 words that come to their mind after visiting. Ask them to be honest. Write these words down and when all the answers are in ask yourself if these words portray the image you want for your studio? If not, re-think your plan and image and get back to work until they do.

A Tool To Make Clients Sessions/Events Available For Viewing And/Or Purchasing

The first generation of on-line proofing came when Hicks Corporation introduced ProShots™, enabling labs to provide photographers with images on CD-ROM or over the Internet instead of, or in addition to, traditional paper proofs. Next, consumer labs began to offer similar services to the public, which combined with software, allowed people to view and share images over the Internet.

And today, companies such as *PhotosAtMyDoor*, *Marathon Press*, *Collages.net*, *Resources.com*, *UpdateSoftware*, *E-Studio*, *PhotoAccess.com*, *and LustreColor* have brought e-commerce technology to professional photographers on their respective websites. Photographers now have an economical and practical way to get images online to share images with clients, and most important, a means by which they could sell their images on-line.

A common mistake made by some photographers early in the Internet era, was to replace their entire sales process with online sales. One must remember the Internet is a great *tool to assist and enhance your business* but not replace your business. Many consumers are not completely ready for absolutely non-human interaction. You will not make nearly the same amount of sales if you depend solely on your website to do the selling.

A Tool To Communicate With Current Or Past Customers

The Internet is an amazing communication tool. If you are online these days you may get several e-mails a day consisting of jokes, letters, business items to discuss etc. Did you ever stop to think that there are some jokes that literally forwarded to hundreds of thousands of people before they got to you! I am not suggesting you start a joke company but the point is clear. Through e-mail people can communicate easily, effectively and FREE! Therefore if you and your business grew and maintained an online database of clients you too could, with the right tools, market to your clients by sending an offer through e-mail for free.

Many photographers know that newsletters are a great way to increase awareness of their business, increase referrals and therefore increase the lifetime value of their clients. "Many photographers nationwide that could never find the time to send newsletters out before are now using our system to send out E-Newsletters. These are simple, fast and best of all Free! Photographers are saving tons of time and saving a lot of money in their marketing budget," said Mr. St. Pierre.

If 6 out of 10 of your customers are online, doesn't it make sense to communicate with them where they there. I am not suggesting that you stop all your other marketing efforts by any means, nor am I suggesting that you pester people with unsolicited (junk) e-mails. Providing opt-in or permission marketing programs[40] for your clients to access incentives, news and other information of interest is more wanted than you would believe and as online presence grows you will find that creating a relationship with people online will drive the lifetime value of your clients through the roof.

A TOOL FOR PHOTOGRAPHERS TO INCREASE REVENUE BY CONDUCTING E-COMMERCE

Today photographers across the country are promoting the viewing and purchasing of photos online and are happily surprised at the way they can increase the average sale. Recently photographers have been making gift certificates and bridal registry's available online.

Combined with a strong marketing effort these E-Commerce tactics are effective. 95% of photographer's websites are "static", meaning they only contain information. Photographers that have E-Commerce such as the ability to buy pictures online, sell gift certificates, etc. create a more engaging positive experience for their client. How many gift certificates do you sell a year? How many clients could you get in your online database in the next 6 months? Imagine if you could send a message (using permission marketing) to hundreds of clients in your database wishing them a happy holiday season from your studio and included an offer such as, "Thinking about a great

---

[40] With Opt-in email, clients ask to be placed on your email distribution list. Names and personal information are never shared with any outside company or vendor.

holiday gift, click this to buy gift certificates from XYZ Photography." Do you think you would sell more gift certificates? You bet! Not only would you sell more gift certificates but also if they had a family portrait in mind, who do you think they will call?

A Tool For Photographers
To Increase Their Marketing Presence By Mass Marketing To Their Clientele Online

The number one rule to marketing is that consumers must see or hear your name 7-8 times before making a decision to call or communicate with your business. If you sent out regular e-newsletters, sent out programmed holiday or birthday wishes, or promoted new events you were running, customers would be more likely to think about you every time the mention of photography came up with friends. You are in a relationship business and there is no better way to communicate with your customers than online and for FREE!

If you are satisfied with your marketing budget, use online tools to enhance your marketing communications. If you want to decrease your marketing budget, build your online database quickly and use it!

The old philosophy that if you build a website and people will show up, is dead! You must promote and leverage your customer database to make the web the most effective tool for your business.

Marketing and Sales

The Old Rules Of Marketing One's Business Become Even More Important On The Web

Whether you market on the web or through more conventional methods to promote your business, you still need to understand what your clients want and which tools will be most effective in delivering those products and services. The Internet is simply a new tool photographers have to market their work and increase sales and profit.

The good news is, having a web presence has never been easier. Web designing software is inexpensive and there is no shortage of companies willing to design your website for as little as a few hundred dollars. Even e-commerce, once limited to large corporations, has become cost effective.

The bad news is, because the cost of entry is so low, people are not always thinking through the process and are either disappointed with the results or they need to spend lots of additional money to correct an earlier decision. To help you avoid the common pitfalls and mistakes associated with the Internet, I sat down with industry experts and asked them to share their thoughts on how photographers can maximize their Internet presence and avoid costly mistakes and errors.

Twelve Steps To A Better Website

Having a web page has become as common as having a fax number—consumers now expect you to have one. But where do you begin? As I noted earlier, web designing software is inexpensive and relatively easy to use and there is no shortage of companies offering to design your web page, some for as little as a few hundred dollars for a simple template-based page to custom-designed website costing well over $5,000. So what is the best course of action?

If there is one area where all marketing/business experts agree, it is on the need to know who your ideal clients are and who they are not. Marketing a web page is no different. Before you invest your time and money in creating a web page, you need to know whom the web page is targeted towards. Who your target audience is will influence your site's look, design, and how it is marketed.

Once you know to whom your web page is aimed, you need to determine what you want them to do once they find you. It sounds simple, but this is a common marketing mistake—one not exclusive to web page design. Consider the following:

- What action do you want people to take when they visit your site?
- Do you want visitors to make a purchase on your site or simply request additional information?
- If you're capturing information, what question(s) will you ask people to answer?
- What information do you want your site to include?
- What are you trying to accomplish?

I asked my website developer (Stephen Simon, Steve Simon Design and Multi-Media) to share with me some tips on what makes a web page work and what mistakes you should avoid. Stephen, who has worked on websites for small businesses as well as sites for large International companies, has a background in graphic design and started his business in 1995. In the Appendix you'll find Stephen's "Twelve Steps to a Better Website" Whether you design your own website or hire someone to do it for you, I think you'll find Stephen's tips invaluable.

WEBPAGE MARKETING DO'S AND DON'TS

O.K., you've invested your time and money to create the perfect web page, now what? That's the question I asked Andrew Cementing, Vice President of Skyworld Internet Services in Waltham, Massachusetts. Skyworld designs and maintains websites for companies all over the world. Andrew also acts as a consultant to companies who may already have a web page, but have been disappointed with the results. Andrew noted that keeping up with how search engines (companies to help people find your web page) is a full-time job. In fact, Skyworld has two full-time employees who do exactly that. Andrew suggests that people consider the following:

Key words and phrases—Each Search Engine looks at things differently. Some rank websites based on Meta tags, others use key words or phrases that potential clients may use to search for your services (Such as: weddings, photographer, children, pets, etc.) Consider using different Meta tags and key words based on what *each search engine* is looking for.

Use text not graphics—Many search engines use the text (not graphics) to determine your listing. For example, a friend told me of a company that was offering to create a website for under $300. I had Steve Simon check out the site and he told me the site placed all the text as a graphic. Search engines will look at the content of your site, for the key words and phrases it uses to rank your site on their service. By placing all the text as a graphic, search engines can't read the text and your site drops to the bottom. If your site is not on the first three pages, no one will find it.

Consider multiple domain names—Since some engines sort alphabetically, having more than one domain name (all linked to the same site) could raise your ranking. Most ISP's (companies that host websites) offer you the option to have multiple domain names. For example, I have multiple domain names including: www.tillphotography.com, www.marktill.comhttp://www.tillphotography.com/, and www.lucrativephotographer.com. All three domain names point to the same website. My ISP charges only $5 per month extra for each additional domain name.

Give people a reason to come back and revisit your site— More and more companies are offering daily, weekly, or monthly specials for their services that are available only on their websites. People need to visit the site regularly to find out what the current special is. Some companies, like Southwest Airlines, email their better clients to remind them to log on and checkout what's new. Other ideas include having a tip of the day. Remember to keep your site fresh and your information current.

Marketing and Sales

Link to related sites—Consider linking your web page to other sites such as local and national professional associations and groups dedicated to marketing to your target audience (some of these sites charge you to link to them). When creating a link, it is important for you make it easy for your visitor to return to your web page. Two common techniques include: Opening the linked site within your site so visitors never really leave and having a "Back To" button on the top of the screen to allow people to return when they're done.

Capture names and addresses—Failing to capture names and addresses of prospects is not exclusive to websites. Consider giving visitors a reason to leave their name and address with you. Offer to give something away for free, such as a report (tips on how to hire a photographer, etc.). Of course, once you have the information, have a plan of action in place to use it.

Everything on the web page should be available in 2-3 clicks of the mouse—Nothing is more frustrating than not being able to find what you want quickly on a website. The public is becoming increasingly impatient when it comes to browsing on the web. For example, people will only wait about 5 seconds (down from 45 seconds) for a page to load up before they move on to another site. Not knowing where they are on the webpage is another thing that frustrates visitors. The bottom-line, make your site user friendly.

Make sure all your collateral material mentions your web address—Would you print a business card and not include your phone number? Of course not, but you would be surprised how often people forget to include their web address. Also, don't forget to mention your site on your voice mail.

ODDS AND ENDS

- Answer your email—All email and requests for information should be responded to within 24 hours.
- Make sure your site allows visitors to take the action you want them to take. Andrew related a story to me of a large company that had spent close to six figures designing a website only to find out visitors could not request any information.

SUMMARY

E-commerce and the Internet have and will continue to change the way we conduct business. Fortunately, getting started has never been simpler or easier. Like any other part of your business, it does take some planning and effort. Apply a little marketing common sense, and you'll quickly see improvements to your bottom line.

RESOURCES

CONSULTANTS
Stephen Simon Multimedia Design, Stephen Simon, 42 Kent Street, #2, Brookline, Massachusetts 02445, (781) 730-5766, ssimon@world.std.com.

Skyworld, Inc., Andrew Deletion, One Moody Street, Waltham, Massachusetts 02453, (781) 893-3600, www.skyworld.com.

JMB Marketing, Bob Martel, 210 Clover Hill Street, Marlborough, Massachusetts 01752-6013, (508) 481-8383, www.info@jmbmarketing.com

COMPANIES

PhotosAtMyDoor, Rich Schiavo, 525 S. 4th Street, Philadelphia, Pennsylvania, 19147-0243, (877) 926-3667, www.photosatmydoor.com.

LustreColor, Ken Wilson, 540 Turnpike Street, Canton, Massachusetts, 02021-2725, (800) 827-7101, www.lustrecolor.com.

Collages.net, 1-877-NET-PHOTO (877-638-7468) or email us at customerservice@collages.net.

UpdateSoftware, Gene Gessert, 4701 Willard Ave, 1508 Chevy Chase, MD 20815, (301) 657 6233, www.updatesoftware.com

The Gift Basket Inc., Lee McGraw and Matt Lewicki, 1500 Main Street, Waltham, Massachusetts 02451-1623, (781) 642-1200.

Black and White Darkroom, Jonathan Penney 176 Main Street, Center Moriches, New York, 11934-1706, (516) 874-3409, www.bwdarkroom.com.

BOOKS

Guerrilla Marketing, Secrets For Making Big Profits From Your Small Business, Jay Conrad Levinson, ©1984 Houghton Mifflin.

The Twenty-Two Immutable Laws Of Branding: How To Build A Product Or Service Into A World-Class Brand, Al Ries and Laura Ries, ©1998, Harper Business.

Marketing and Sales

Direct Marketing Success, What Works and Why, Freeman F. Gosden, Jr., ©1985, John Wiley and Sons, Inc.

Business By Referral, A Sure-Fire Way to Generate New Business, Ivan R. Misner, Ph.D. & Robert Davis, ©1998 Bard Press

The World's Best Known Marketing Secret, Building Your Business by Word-Of-Mouth Marketing, Ivan R. Misner, Ph.D., ©1994 Bard & Stephen

Raving Fans, A Revolutionary Approach to Customer Service, ©1993, Ken Blanchard and Sheldon Bowles, William Morrow and Co.

Customers For Life: How To Turn That One-Time Buyer Into A Lifetime Customer. Carl Sewell, ©1990, Pocket Books.

Endless Referrals: Network Your Everyday Contacts Into Sales, Bob Burg, ©1994, McGraw-Hill

Knock Your Socks Off Service Recovery, Ron Zemke & Chip R. Bell, ©2000, Amazon Books

1,001 Ways to Keep Customers Coming Back: Wow Ideas That Make Customers Happy and Increase Your Bottom Line, Ted Kinni and Donna Greiner, ©1999 Prima Publishing

Marketing with Newsletters, How To Boost Sales, Add Members, Raise Donations, And Further Your Cause With A Promotional Newsletter, by Elaine Floyd, ©1992 Newsletter Resources.

ORGANIZATIONS

Business Network International, 268 S. Bucknell Ave. Claremont, California, 91711-4907, (800) 825-8286 or (909) 624-2227

Marketing and Sales

Protecting Your Assets

☞ Legal Considerations
☞ What If?
☞ Backup Equipment
☞ Financial Planning
☞ Is Your Studio A Good Investment?
☞ Buying Or Selling A Studio

Legal Considerations

The world today is one of laws and regulations. Photographers are not immune from dealing with this aspect of their business. Some laws protect the photographer and others require compliance. Yet it may be the legal system itself that is the most frightening aspect of doing business as a photographer.

THE LEGAL SYSTEM

Imagine you photographed a wedding in a professional manner. The bride ordered a 66-page album containing over 140 images. When the mother of the bride saw the bill, she became enraged saying these were the worst photos she had ever seen. She hired an attorney seeking to obtain the album, the proofs, and the negatives without paying.

Sound far-fetched? It actually happened to Laura and me. I relate this story because it shows that being a business owner is not without risk. Even if you do everything correctly, you can be sued. This is why you need to make sure you are adequately compensated, not just for your time and talent, but also for the added liability of being a business owner.

The reality in today's marketplace is that people are much more willing to sue, whether or not the facts in the case support the legal action. I was fortunate that I was a Professional Photographer of America (PPA) member. Part of the membership dues goes towards an indemnification trust that covers these situations. Had it not been for the insurance coverage, I may very well have been forced to settle on less than favorable terms. As it turned out, I had an excellent attorney and my client essentially got nothing.

One of the reasons the PPA coverage is so comprehensive is because it is carefully drafted to cover the things that will happen to photographers. Most commercial policies are expensive with limited coverage. Many people have had commercial liability coverage in effect at the time they were sued only to find out that their policy would not cover their specific situation. Of course the PPA policy does not cover every situation, but I would not be a photographer without it.

In the event that you are sued, put your insurer carrier on notice of the claim ASAP to avoid the potential loss of coverage. Your behavior toward your client and your attempts to correct whatever went wrong count a lot. If you acted in a fair and reasonable way without admitting fault, you can undermine, to some extent, the plaintiff's claim. Do not admit fault. Doing so can give the plaintiff ammunition that can be used against you.

THE DANGERS OF SUBCONTRACTING ASSIGNMENTS

It is a common practice in our industry to subcontract assignments to other photographers. The practice is not without risk. Whether or not you do the actual photography, as the studio owner you are liable for the actions of your employees and contractors. Hiring other photographers is not a problem. But if these individuals are not PPA members, your studio will not be covered under your PPA indemnification policy.

Even though you may be covered, they are not. If your studio is sued, you may have to pay for your legal defense out of your own pocket.

I suggest that you hire only photographers who are PPA members. If they are full-time employees, you can add them to your policy. If you subcontract the help, verify with the PPA directly, that their policy is in effect.

There are also copyright issues that arise regarding ownership of the photographs taken by an independent contractor. You should make sure that the independent contractor and you have a written agreement on the ownership and use of the images and the copyrights. Additionally there are potentially serious tax issues for both the contractor and the studio when an independent contractor relationship is used. Work with an attorney and an accountant to comply with IRS rules.

AN OUNCE OF PREVENTION, A POUND OF CURE

The best way you can protect yourself is with a well-written contract. Consider the following:

- A schedule that will tell you in a detailed way anything specific the client will want
- A sentence that limits damage to refund of deposits (it won't save you in the case of negligence)
- The names of the parties
- Signatures of all parties
- The time frame for completing the work
- The dollar amount of the contract

Good documentation is a good practice from both a business and legal perspective. We have clients initial the contract that they have read our terms and conditions as well as sign a separate terms and conditions contract. I figure if they sign the contract, initial the contract, and sign a separate terms and conditions statement, the one thing they can't claim afterwards is, "I never told them...."

Of course, good documentation is not a substitute for quality work and treating your clients fairly and honestly. However, in case doing a good job is not enough, it can go a long way.

COPYRIGHT ISSUES

Technology has decreased the cost of illegal copying and increased the quality of the copies that clients and others can make of our copyrighted photographs. Ownership of copyrights can sometimes be an issue. While the complexity of these issues is beyond the scope of this book, you should be aware of:

- Client's copying and scanning your prints (this is not always innocent).
- Seniors ordering the cheapest package knowing that they will scan and print copies for friends.
- Copying centers facilitating the violation of your copyrights (and even displaying how those prints can be copied by their center at a fraction of the cost).
- Clients exceeding the rights that were granted to them (e.g. a license is granted to use a print for

brochures and your print improperly shows up on a billboard).

- Other photographers copying printed materials that your studio developed (e.g. a planning package that cost you thousands of dollars to have professionally written).
- The media copying "newsworthy" prints claiming "fair use" at your expense.
- TV documentaries using prints obtained from the family without your permission.
- Clients exceeding their right to display your prints by publishing the prints electronically (purchasing prints does not necessarily grant the client a right to publish the same print on a web site).
- The right of privacy and the right of publicity that diminishes what may be perceived as a right that goes with a copyright (e.g. a failure to get a model release sufficient to protect the studio's intended use).
- Copying of prints off of your website.
- Independent contractors owning copyrights

Most of the time, planning and attention to details can adequately handle these issues. The first line of defense is to include a section on copyrights in your planning package. This should be followed by a discussion of copyrights with ever client, every time you do work for them. If you intend to allow a client limited use (type of use, format, time, or quantity of use), you should spell this out in writing. Posted copyright policies in the studio will reinforce these concepts.

The Lucrative Photographer

Although under the current law every original work is copyrighted from the time that it is affixed in tangible form, the public still has a perception that it is only copyrighted if there is a copyright notice. Because of this and because of the opportunity to notify your clients and the world of your copyright, every print should have a copyright notice on it.

Next, consider registering your works with the U.S. Copyright Office. A copyright violation of a registered work may afford you not only the right to actual damages but statutory damages (ranging from $500 to $20,000 and in some cases, $100,000 depending upon the circumstances) plus attorney's fees.

As of August 16, 2001, the U.S. Copyright office accepts Group Registration of prints. You can now register groups of photographs taken within the same calendar year for a single $30 fee. You have to deposit the photographs with the copyright office but a "deposit" can take many forms (e.g. a video tape, electronic images on a CD, photocopies, and slides containing up to 36 images). A Group Registration can only be used if the same photographer photographed all images forming that registration. You must keep track of the dates of publication and list them on the registration form for each print. Alternatively, you can register all of your prints approximately every three months if you want to use a single range of dates not exceeding three months preceding the date of registration. While there are a number of technical requirements for Group Registration, after you have registered a group once or twice, you will develop a procedure that will make the process easy.

Protecting Your Assets

Ultimately, your prints WILL be illegally copied. Therefore, you should develop a plan for dealing with this inevitability. It is one thing if your best client scanned a print to send to grandma and another thing when wedding portraits are copied and sent electronically to every attendee at a wedding or incorporated into thank you cards without your permission. Again, this plan should be formulated and discussed with clients.

ELECTRONIC RIGHTS

The Internet and digital images pose many opportunities and challenges for the photographer. A short list of some of the issues may be a start to electronically expanding your market base with a degree of practical and legal protections:

- Do you want to have a web site? If so, who will own the copyrights to the site, you or the web site developer? What if you want to have your site modified by a different developer?
- How will you protect your images? Low-resolution prints? Protection software that prevents copying that ranges from inexpensive to very expensive? A "copyright" watermark imbedded in crucial places on each image?
- Will you e-mail prints to clients and their family for viewing and ordering? How will you protect digital copying of these prints?
- Is there a marketing plan that makes sense to you that includes providing digital images to clients on a CD?

The Lucrative Photographer

- Is a commercial, third party marketing website compatible with your marketing plans?
- If you sell your studio, your model releases may not be transferable.

Again, the practical approach is indispensable. However, there are remedies short of litigation in many cases. For example, the Digital Millenniums Copyright Act of 1998 provides a number of remedies favorable to the photographer. For example, if you find out that one of your prints is being displayed without your permission on a website, the Act provides a procedure for notifying the website server to remove the copyrighted prints. The server could then be liable to you if the print is not removed.

Don't be afraid of the electronic-digital age of photography. However, learn about the risks and rewards.

Your Own Copyright Infringement
Copyright laws protect the person who creates an original work. Photographers frequently violate the rights of others, which can create a completely different set of problems. Consider:

- Are you using music with your slide or computer presentations? If so, you may need a license (generally from BMI or ASCAP).
- Do you play music during a sitting? Depending on the size of your studio, you may need a license.
- Do you have a license for each copy of software loaded on each of your computers?

- Have you ever taken a photograph that includes another photograph as a substantial part of your print?
- How about photographing architecture that is not readily visible or photographing a sculpture?

If you are in the business of creativity, consider the rights that others have in their creative works. Equally important, consider the liabilities that you may incur by not respecting the rights of others.

TRADEMARKS

More and more photographers recognize the importance of brand identification of their products. To facilitate this, trademarks in the nature of a studio name and/or a logo are being developed. A trademark is an audio, visual, or other mark that associates the product with the origin or creator of the product. You should be careful not to infringe on the mark of another photographer. Acquaint yourself with the various ways to obtain a trademark (common law, state registration, and federal registration). Once a mark is obtained, it must be policed in order to protect the mark. This can be a complicated legal area, but an important one for some photographers – particularly if there is more than one studio location.

EMPLOYEES

You should prepare a contract of employment for every employee. It is simply a way to set forth expectations and attempt to avoid problems. Consider vacation time (when it is earned and when it can be taken) and sick leave. Under what circumstances can the employee be terminated (this could avoid an unemployment compensation claim or worse, a wrongful termination claim)? What about their use of your computers, equipment, e-mail, Internet use and copying or loading computer programs? These issues can actually be addressed in a three-page contract.

ADVICE

While all of this may seem daunting, the Lucrative Photographer is one who artistically creates photographs and pragmatically runs a business. A little time with an attorney and an accountant is generally money well spent.

What If?

Imagine sitting down to watch the evening news and seeing that a nearby office building had been destroyed by fire. The story hit home when I saw the face of a fellow photographer being interviewed by the press. His studio was located in the building and he barely escaped with his life. All of his life's work was left behind and was lost in the fire. All of his equipment, his negatives, client albums, and computer records—gone in a matter of minutes. Sadly, this scenario was repeated a month or so later when another photographer in our area also lost his studio to a fire.

These are not hypothetical examples—each story happened within several months of each other. I share these stories because it is easy to think that something like this can't happen to us. Unfortunately, more often than not business owners do not take the necessary precautions to adequately protect their business and minimize their losses.

The loss of two photographers' studios made me take a look at my preparedness. I contacted my friend and insurance professional Mike Norman (Aronson Insurance, Newton, MA 617-965-3030) to discuss what types of coverage business owners should have. Before I begin, I would like to say that the purpose of this section is NOT to provide insurance advice. Rather, it is designed to help you think about your own situation. If you have any questions regarding what type of coverage you should have, please contact your insurance professional.

Loss of Data

The first thing many people think about in a catastrophic loss such as fire is replacing their equipment—which is a good idea. However, a contingency plan discussion would not be complete without addressing computer data. In today's high-tech environment, losing ones data can be more serious than the equipment itself.

Many business owners backup their data on a regular basis, but leave the backup copy in the same place as the computer. You may want to make more than one copy of critical data—one on-site, the other off-site. This enables you to keep several copies of your data and rotate among different backup sets when you make subsequent backups. Also, should one of your disks become damaged, you will still be able to retrieve your data. If your studio is not in your home, bring the backup disks home with you. If this is not an option consider leaving a copy with a friend. There are also services that allow you to backup your data over the Internet.

Off-site backups are crucial! Always store a set off-site to guard against fire, theft, and natural disasters. The following backup tips will help you ensure the security of your data and possibly the survival of your business.

Backup Methods

There are two basic ways to backup your data: 1) Transfer data to a portable disk and physically take the backup disk off-site to a secure location, or 2) Use an Internet backup company (like Dantz) to create instant off-site backup for your critical files.

225

HOW DO I SET UP A
TRADITIONAL MEDIA ROTATION SCHEDULE?

If you backup your data to a portable disk, experts recommend that you use multiple disks and rotate each disk's use on either a daily or weekly schedule. There are software programs (such as Retrospect) that will automate this function for you. Personally, I prefer a daily backup system. If you get into the habit of backing up your data daily, you're less likely to forget and of course there is less data that can be lost. I use a tip I received from PC consultant, Steve Sotsky, Framingham, Massachusetts. Steve recommends having five backup disks. Label each disk for each of the five business days of the week (Monday through Friday). If your business is open six or seven days each week you'll want to have more disks. At the end of each business day insert the correct media into your backup drive on the appropriate day, backup the data, and (most importantly) take the backup disk off-site. If offsite backup is not possible or practical, consider backing up your data via the Internet.

BACKUP VIA THE INTERNET

Instead of copying your data to removable media and physically taking the media off-site, you can now perform the same function using the Internet. Internet backup sites are growing in popularity, particularly for those individuals who use laptop computers and are away from their offices on a regular basis. The advantage is that you can back up and restore your data anywhere you have an Internet connection. Backing up to an FTP (File Transfer Protocol) site over the Internet is just like backing up to disk or tape sets. It is important to choose a vendor that hosts a site specially selected to provide you with fast, secure, and inexpensive Internet storage space.

To ensure backups remain secure, it is recommended that you use software with an encryption feature to process the data before it's sent out onto the Internet. Even if someone could intercept it, they couldn't decipher it without your encryption key. Also, backup sites should provide secure servers to store your data, so no one has access to it.

Backing up data to the web is as fast as your connection will allow. You may wish to compress your data prior to uploading. Compression will typically shrink your files to anywhere from three-quarters to one-half of their original size for faster uploading. People I know that have used similar systems report that backup can take several hours and is usually done at night.

SELECT AND BACK UP CRITICAL FILES

Experts recommend your backups should include all of your files. Complete backups make restoring your system after a disaster much faster, easier, and more secure. While you can back up all your files, you may want to select only critically important files such as databases, tax records, accounts receivable, or presentations.

You may want to make more than one copy of critical data—one on-site, the other off-site. This enables you to keep several copies of your data and rotate among different backup sets when you make subsequent backups. Also, should one of your disks become damaged, you will still be able to retrieve your data.

BACKUP POWER SUPPLIES

While use of surge protectors to prevent computer damage from lightening and other power surges has become common, protection against drops in power is often overlooked. Particularly in the summer months when demand for power is at its peak, dips in power are common. If your computer is performing a task when the power drops you could lose data, or even damage your machine. Fortunately, backup power supplies (referred to as UPC's) are inexpensive ($250-$350). These devices automatically kick in when it detects the slightest drop in power. Often I will hear it chirp (indicating it went on) without noticing any flickering of the lights or other indication of a drop in power. A backup power supply is a classic example of an ounce of prevention versus a pound of cure.

PREVENTIVE MAINTENANCE

Once again I have assembled a panel of experts to assist me in providing you with helpful tips and ideas. My computer consultants are Howard Hillman, HDH Associates, and Steve Sotsky. I asked them to give me a list of tips to help you keep your computers running at peak efficiency and avoid common pitfalls.

Run scan disk (PC) or disk first aid (Mac)—at least once per week. Utilities such as Norton Disk Doctor and others perform similar, and sometimes, more thorough testing. These programs are designed to test and fix glitches that occur from day to day use of your computer. Keeping up with these "repairs" can prevent more serious problems down the road. An analogy would be a minor tune-up for your car.

Clean out temporary files regularly—Each time you use your computer, it creates temporary files as it works. Deleting temporary files improves your computer's performance.

Use anti-virus software—If you don't have Anti-Virus software on your computer, order it today. Most of us are constantly downloading programs and files from the Internet and/or sharing disks with fellow photographers and service bureaus. Programs such as Norton Anti-Virus and McAffee Anti-Virus do an excellent job in catching potential problems.

Update software—All software manufacturers offer updates (both increased features and bug fixes) on their websites. Some companies such as Norton or Intuit let you access the updates from within the programs themselves. Make a habit of regularly checking all your software sites to see if updates are available.

Create an emergency boot disk (PC)—Most utility programs will assist you in creating a disk that will allow you to start up your computer if your main hard drive has failed or your startup software has become corrupted. (Macintosh computers can use programs such as Norton Utilities and TechTools that include an operating system on the program CD.) If you use your computer long enough, you will eventually need this feature; don't wait until it's too late.

Protecting Your Assets

Read trade journals—Magazines such as *MacWorld, PCWorld, PC Magazine,* etc. offer a wealth of information on helpful tips, bug fixes, and neat shortcuts. Make a habit of reading these journals to stay up to speed.

Don't be afraid to get some help—I am fortunate to have access to people like Howard and Steve. They have saved me on more than one occasion. Make friends with folks like them.

BUSINESS INTERRUPTION INSURANCE

Loss of data is only one area of concern. Business interruption insurance is used to cover loss of income and/or additional expenses that arise if your business suffers a loss due to damage covered in your property insurance policy. There are two basic types of coverage.

- *Business Income Insurance*—is used for companies whose business will be shut down for an extended period of time, such as a restaurant. For companies such as these, it is not practical or possible for the business to open up in a temporary location during the rebuilding process. The policy should pay your salary, the salary of your key employees, profits, and all ongoing expenses while you rebuild. The key factor is that loss must be due to something covered in the property insurance policy itself. If your property insurance policy covers losses due to fire and you have a fire, you are covered. If the loss is due to an earthquake and you don't have earthquake insurance, the loss is not covered.

- *Extra Expense Insurance*—is designed for businesses that must remain open, such as a wedding photographer. The business could operate out of a temporary location while you rebuild. The policy should pay the *additional expenses* associated with operating out of a temporary location.

Business interruption insurance covers your losses, but what if you were responsible for the loss, such as a spray booth fire. If you are a tenant in a building you don't own, you may have some liability to reimburse the damage caused to the other tenants; however, *Fire legal liability insurance* may be necessary to cover any damage to the portion of the building you occupy.

PROPERTY INSURANCE

Property Insurance—protects you and your business from financial loss stemming from direct damage to:

- *Your property*—such as buildings you own, inventory, furniture and fixtures, supplies, equipment, money, etc.
- *Property of others*—for which you may be responsible such as leased equipment and customer goods left in your care. An example of property left in our care might include a one-of-a kind photo for you to restore, merchandise to photograph; wedding albums that are complete and paid for. You need to determine if your policy will cover you under these circumstances.
- *Inland Marine policy*—One thing that is not covered by many property insurance policies is equipment located off-site. When you take your equipment to photograph a wedding, a family at the beach, or to

a commercial location you will need what is referred to as an *Inland Marine policy* to ensure your equipment is protected. It is important to be sure your policy is for the *replacement value* of your equipment.

Insurance to value requirements—most policies require you to cover *all* of your property. If you own $50,000 in personal (non-real estate) property, you may be required to insure the entire amount. There are exceptions, so you should check with your insurance professional. Failure to meet this requirement could have a negative impact on your ability to collect against your claim.

ADDITIONAL COVERAGE

Workers Compensation—laws governing workers compensation insurance requirement vary from state to state. You should check with your insurance professional to determine whether this coverage is applicable.

Liability Insurance—policies provide coverage for third party claims brought against you, your company, or your employees (acting on your behalf). The most common example is someone tripping over a piece of your equipment or falling on your property and sustaining an injury due to your negligence. The policies, in addition to paying claims, often will cover associated legal bills.

Another area of coverage is *professional malpractice*, also known as Errors & Omissions. These policies protect you against lawsuits brought against you by your clients for negligence relating to your completing the photographic assignment. The good news is your PPA dues include coverage under the PPA's indemnification trust. While the coverage is very good, you owe it to yourself to review the coverage to make sure you are adequately protected.

BACKUP EQUIPMENT

Vendors will love me for this section. Murphy's Law says, "What can go wrong, will go wrong, at the most inopportune time." Being a wedding photographer, I have had equipment fail during a processional, during formal portraits, when the bride and groom were being introduced into the room, etc. Now you might say, I need better equipment, but anyone who has been in this business for any significant period of time will tell you ALL equipment fails; it's just a matter of when and where.

The good news in all these years, I never missed a key moment because I bring lots of backup equipment with me. (I have the sore back and shoulders to prove it.) For example, I bring three camera bodies (medium format) and two 35mm camera bodies when I do photojournalistic candids. In addition I bring ten film backs, and two of my main lenses, and four flash units. Do I use every one at every event? Of course not, but I have needed to use each and every piece from time to time.

Why do I bring so much? How can I tell a bride I won't be able to photograph all or part of her wedding because I don't have enough equipment? If you were having surgery, would you go to a hospital that didn't have emergency generators to kick-in if the power failed? Being professional means being prepared. Part of being prepared is having the equipment available in case an emergency occurs. I have a complete second camera setup assembled at all times during the wedding. Having the spare camera in my car or unassembled, does me no good.

If you're just starting out in the business, you probably won't be able to have all the equipment I bring. It took me several years to build up to this level. It is a sound business practice to live by the old saying, "An ounce of prevention is worth a pound of cure."

SUMMARY

If you haven't reviewed your backup plans or insurance coverage lately, now is great time. Get in the habit of backing up your data daily and taking the disks off-site. Make sure your insurance coverage is adequate for your needs. The very survival of your business may depend on it because you never know, what if?

Financial Planning

With a background in Investments and Financial Services, financial planning is something that is near and dear to my heart. However, I have been retired from the business for quite sometime, so I sought the advice of a life-long friend (and my financial advisor) Jim Wolfson. Jim is a Certified Financial Planner at Baystate Financial Services, in Boston, Massachusetts. I asked Jim to outline the common mistakes people make in planning for their financial futures and what advice he would give to potential clients to make sound financial plans.

COMMON FINANCIAL PLANNING MISTAKES

According to Jim, people generally fall into two categories: People in the first category tend not to treat financial planning with the same reverence as they do their current day-to-day expenses. People get a paycheck (or owner's draw) and try to pay their current bills. After paying the bills there is either nothing left over (or maybe even a shortfall), or people are too timid to put away the rest for fear they will need it in the near future.

People in the second category do put money away, but not enough to be relevant. For example, let's say you're planning for retirement. Your current age is 45, you have $100,000 saved already, and your goal is to have a retirement income at age 65 of $30,000 (the average income of a photographer). You are currently saving $2,000 each year in an IRA Account. Will you have accumulated enough money by the time you reach age 65? Let's take a look:

As you can see, even though you are contributing $2,000 each year, you will be short of your annual income goal by $5,300. To reach your target goal of $30,000, assuming all other factors remain the same, you will need to increase your annual retirement contribution to $4,946 a year.

RETIREMENT PLANNING PROJECTIONS[41]	
Current Savings Information	*Values*
Current Savings	$100,000
Annual Investment Return	10%
Current Tax Rate	28%
Annual Contribution	$2,000
Predicted Inflation	4%
Retirement Information	*Values*
Current Age	45
Retirement Age	65
Withdraw until age	85
Retirement Income	*$24,706*

Jim's scenarios are supported by my survey. Only 69% of photographers surveyed have a retirement plan, and I would venture to guess that a significant number of those who responded in the affirmative have a plan from a source other than photography. Of those who do have a plan only 27% contribute the maximum

---

[41] Quicken Retirement Financial Calculator

amount allowed each year. In other words, they are under funding their retirement.

According to Jim, the solution is to look at what your GOALS are first. Once you have established your goals, you can go back and develop an action plan. It may be your goals are not obtainable in the time frame you have allotted. In which case, you will either need to lower your goal, extend the time frame, or find a way to generate more income. Listing your goals allows you to make positive decisions. If not, life tends to make the decisions for you, and you may not like the options it chooses.

HOW TO GET STARTED

If you are computer savvy, you should pick up a copy of either Quicken Financial Planner (with Quicken Deluxe) or Microsoft Money, Jim recommends. These software programs enable most people to relate their goals to what is possible based on reasonable assumptions. For instance, you have a two-year-old child and you want to send him or her to Harvard in 16 years. (Harvard is currently well over $30,000 per year based on room, board, tuition, books, etc.). These programs will tell you how much you will need to set aside each year, taking into account inflation and reasonable rate of return on your investments, to reach your goal. The program can also indicate how much help you will need to reach your goals.

WHAT TYPE OF HELP IS AVAILABLE?

There are basically two options available to most people, Jim says—on-going help and periodic help. On-going help involves having one's assets professionally managed and is typically reserved for those who have *Investment Assets in excess of $150,000*. The size of their portfolios necessitates more frequent attention.

The other option is what Jim refers to as periodic help. With this option, a financial plan is developed either by the client or with the assistance of a financial planner. Once the plan is developed, clients should have a yearly "checkup" to make sure the plan is progressing according to schedule.

Which type of plan is right for you will be based in part on the size of your portfolio and how much you are willing to invest in time on your own.

WHAT DOES A FINANCIAL PLAN COVER?

As you might surmise, a financial plan begins with establishing your *Primary Goal*. It might be saving for your children's education, becoming a full-time photographer, or saving for retirement. Once you establish your primary goal, you will want to establish secondary goals. Your goals will be the basis for the remainder of your plan.

The second part of the plan is *Insurance*. Insurance includes life, health, disability, general liability, equipment insurance, etc. As I mentioned earlier, only 40% of photographers have disability insurance covering their photographic income. Unfortunately, in today's economic environment, individual disability insurance is expensive and difficult to come by. The good news is group disability insurance is available through professional associations like the Professional Photographers of America.

Taxes are next. More specifically, how can you pay less in taxes? If you are going to save money for retirement, you can place money in an IRA that reduces your current income. On a $2,000 contribution, that's a potential $560 savings in your tax liability. Talk with your accountant and financial planner during the year to look for ways to reduce your taxes and keep more of what you earn.

Investments are fourth. Which investment vehicles to use and what type of risk you're willing to accept is a function of all three steps above. Generally, the closer you are to your goal's target date, the safer you want the investment to be. Unfortunately, an investment is where many people start. They get a call from an investment broker, read about a hot stock, and start investing without thinking about the implications the investment will have on their plan (if they even have one). You wouldn't set your exposure without knowing what film you are going to use or the lighting conditions you will be photographing with, would you?

If it hasn't been covered by your primary goal, *Retirement Planning* is the fifth step. Going back to the notion of not putting enough money away, people often have no idea how much money they will need at retirement. The financial software mentioned earlier can help you determine your retirement needs.

The last step is *Estate Planning*. A basic estate-planning package includes: wills, power of attorney, health care proxy, and a homestead act (if you own your own home). In most instances, a basic estate-planning package will run approximately $1,000.

MONEY FOR A RAINY DAY

An often-overlooked part of financial planning is having an emergency fund. Most planners will recommend two to three months' salary (after taxes). This fund is for unplanned expenses and is a cushion—a fudge factor of sorts. To build up your emergency fund, set up a money market account (you can write checks but the minimum amount is high, typically $250 - $500) and have money automatically transferred to the account each month. In a relatively short period of time, the account will build to the necessary level. Once the desired balance is attained, continue to deposit some money into the account to keep up with inflation and your increase in salary.

SUMMARY

There's an old saying, "people don't plan to fail they fail to plan." Throughout this book I have stressed over and over the importance of having a plan. Only 5% of the people in the world have a written financial plan, yet they control over 50% of the world's wealth. When I was in the financial services industry, I saw too many people who didn't save enough while they were working to enjoy their retirement. The United States today still has one of the lowest savings rates of any of the industrialized nations. Lucrative photographers know better. Start your plan yesterday.

Is Your Studio A Good Investment?

In January 2000, *The Boston Globe* listed the Boston area companies that provided their investors with the biggest return on their investment (ROI) during the 1990's. The number one Boston area business was EMC Corp., based in Hopkinton, Massachusetts, which had an astounding 72,000% increase in the stock's value in this decade! In English it means that if you invested $1,000 in their stock in 1990, your investment would be worth approximately $7.2 million in the year 2000!

Although the stock market has backed off from its stratospheric levels, I thought it would be interesting to see how the return on your studio investment is doing relative to the rest of the world. Granted, a photography studio is not going to provide the same return on investment as companies such as EMC. However in deciding to own your own business, you are investing your money (and time) in a company and it is appropriate to know what type of return on your investment you can (and should) expect.

This raises an interesting question. Are you better off purchasing equipment to open a studio or would you be better off investing the money elsewhere? Let's take a look.

Let's assume you have $25,000 to invest and you plan to retire in 25 years. Each year you plan to make additional investments (equipment purchases) of $2,500. According to the investment advisors I spoke with, it is reasonable to assume that you could expect to receive a return on your investment of about 10% on average.

However, investing in a business in many ways is a riskier proposition than investing in the stock market as a whole. As a business owner your goal is not to do as good as the market, but to do better, rewarding yourself for the added risk you have as a business owner. Consequently, a return on investment of 12% or 15% or more would be considered reasonable. Let's look at how our "investment" in our studio would look if we were to view it in traditional investment terms.

BUSINESS AS AN INVESTMENT			
Assumptions:	*10% ROI*	*12% ROI*	*15% ROI*
Initial investment	$25,000	$25,000	$25,000
Annual investments	$2,500	$2,500	$2,500
Number of years	25	25	25
Total Investment	$87,500	$87,500	$87,500
Inflation	4%	4%	4%
Investment results[42]			
Value in 25 years	$516,735	$758,336	$1,354,956
Gross profit	$429,235	$670,836	$1,267,456
Final year's interest	$51,674	$91,000	$203,243
Interest in today's dollars	$19,041	$33,533	$74,893

---

[42] Results calculated using Quicken™ investment calculator

The Lucrative Photographer

Thanks to the magic of compound interest, our total investment of $87,500 (over the 25 years) grows to $516,000 at a 10% ROI, to over $1.3 million at 15%. The interest you would earn alone in year 25 is $91,000 at the 12% level.

In business terms, the interest earned in the example above would be equivalent to your studio's profit—what is left over after you have paid all of your bills *and your salary*. In today's dollars (accounting for inflation), $91,000 of studio profit would be approximately $34,200. If studio profit were 12% of sales, a studio would need to generate gross sales of at least $285,000. This is greater than 80% of all studios responding to the Census 2000. The interest alone ($34,200) exceeds the average photographer's salary ($27,000) by 25%.

IMPLICATIONS

Does this mean that owning a photography studio is a poor investment? No, I know several studios whose "investment return" would meet or exceed the example above. However, it does mean that many photographers need to re-evaluate how they view their business. By looking at your business in investment terms, it forces you to strive to create a lucrative business worthy of investing your hard-earned money and time in.

Buying or Selling a Studio

A discussion on running a lucrative studio would not be complete without mentioning valuing your business—how much is it really worth? Many photographers operate on the assumption that they will be able to sell their business at a premium based on their sweat equity and goodwill and live happily ever after.

Leonard Levy, M.Photog.Cr., has lectured throughout the US, Mexico, and Canada on business and photography, having run a lucrative studio of his own for many years. Len has also made a career helping photographers buy and sell studios. According to Len, it is very difficult to sell a successful photography studio and keep it thriving after the sale, because photography is such a personalized service. Oftentimes the person buying the business does not have the necessary business or photographic skills required to ensure the studio's continued success. Consequently, the failure rate of a studio after the sale is high. A studio owner who originally thought he or she had sold a thriving business may end up taking back a less than successful studio.

Len related a story of a photographer who sold his very successful studio to an individual, who, for a variety of reasons, couldn't keep the studio solvent. Subsequently, the original photographer had to take over the building where the studio used to be, fix it up, and sell the building. The original photographer was fortunate that the building sold for more than the money the seller owed him. However, it could have easily gone the other way. The building could have sold for less than the amount the photographer owed, or worse, the necessity for the seller to take over the business at a time when he/she could ill afford to do so. Does this mean that selling a studio is a bad idea? No, it does mean that before you sell or buy, you need to do your homework.

WHAT IS A STUDIO WORTH?

So how do you evaluate a studio's worth? Len says that before you buy a studio you should look at the cost and determine how long it will take to recover the purchase price as compared to taking the money and simply investing it. It could be that investing your money is the better choice. Assuming the purchase or sale of the studio is a sound idea, how much is the studio worth?

"The purchase price of a business is based in part on how it will be financed," says Jack M. Murray, Jr., CBA, who is Vice President—Director of Audit and Risk Management at Danvers Savings Bank, Danvers, Massachusetts. Common methods used to assess the value of a business include the company's yearly gross sales, net profit, or some combination of the two. While it is common in other industries for lucrative businesses to sell for 100% (or more) of the prior year's gross sales, photography studios often sell for only 60-65% of sales or less. One reason, as Len points out, is that the seller typically does not have an existing mortgage on the business. As a result, the seller's take-home pay can be considerably larger than what the potential buyer would earn (at least in the short run),

245

since the buyer has the added expense of a business mortgage.

FINANCING A STUDIO PURCHASE

Let's assume you want to buy a studio that has gross sales of $250,000 and shows that the owner had salary and benefits totaling $70,000. The agreed selling price was 60% of sales or $150,000 with tangible assets of $75,000. If the buyer puts 20% down ($30,000), he or she is left with a business mortgage of $120,000. To obtain financing from a bank, you will need to prove that the business can generate enough positive cash flow to pay off the loan.

STUDIO PURCHASE ILLUSTRATION	
Gross Sales	$250,000
Owner's Salary	$70,000
Tangible Assets	$75,000
Net Income (10% of Sales)	$25,000
Depreciation	$25,000
Net Selling Price	$150,000
Down Payment (20%)	$30,000
Business Mortgage	$120,000
Term (10% for 10 years)	
Monthly Payment	$1,586
Inc. needed for debt service (Pmt. * 1.5)	$2,379
Mo. Net Income plus depreciation	$4,167

Business loans from banks typically do not extend past ten years. Assuming a 10% interest rate, the monthly business mortgage payment for your studio purchase would be $1,586 for ten years. Before the seller buys the business, the bank needs to be assured that the studio can generate enough income not only to pay the normal overhead and cost of goods sold, but also the business mortgage *as well as having enough money left over for a reasonable salary for the owner.* Jack notes that banks look for a positive debt service ratio of 1.3 to 1.5 times the debt service. In English, if your business mortgage is $1,586 per month, the bank will want to see the business generate a positive cash flow of $2,200 to $2,400 per month (after all operating expenses, including salary). The reason is fairly straightforward; the bank wants to have a little cushion. If the business can't generate that kind of cash, you will need either to put more money down, to lower the purchase price, or walk away.

The bank will also want some sort of collateral (tangible assets) to secure the loan. That means if you default, the bank can take possession of the assets and sell them to pay off your debt. This is why Len recommends that tangible assets equal at least 50% of the selling price. You will need the collateral to secure the loan. However, the bank may ask for additional collateral, such as a second mortgage on your home to make up any difference.

Jack also notes that banks will want see at least three years of financial statements and federal tax returns from the existing business, a Performa income statement projecting how you see the business performing, your personal financial statements, and a solid business plan on how you will make it all work.

Protecting Your Assets

It is easy to understand why a bank would think this way if we look at buying a studio, not as a place for us to work, but rather as an investment. Suppose we buy a studio and instead of working there ourselves, we hire the photographers and pay someone to manage the day-to-day operations. We would expect the studio to generate enough money to pay all the bills, including the loan payments and still have enough money left over for us as investors. This way of thinking requires you to approach your profession as a business rather than a paid hobby.

VALUE BASED ON "TIMES EARNINGS"

Another way to assess a studio's worth is to look at its net income and basing the purchase price on the studio's *real profit*. Using this valuation method, a good rule of thumb is to value studios at approximately three times real earnings.

Conducting an extensive financial review is essential regardless of which business evaluation model you chose. As a former internal auditor and financial advisor, I know that small business owners like to use "creative accounting" methods to understate their company's true financial picture. If the owner is incorporated, there may be a tax benefit for the business *not to show a profit*, or if it does, only a small one. Also, it is not uncommon for a business owner to co-mingle personal and business. Only an extensive financial review will unveil a studio's true financial condition. This type of review requires a trained professional, such as a CPA. The fees for such a review are well worth the expense.

The Lucrative Photographer

Len Levy believes that work-in-progress is the biggest sticking point in negotiating the selling price. The sale price needs to be adjusted to account for deposits held for jobs in various stages of completion. According to both men, work-in-progress can be broken down into the following categories:

Deposits taken for jobs not photographed—In this case the *deposits belong to the buyer.*

Finished work is complete and money has been paid in advance—Consists of finished work that is waiting to be delivered to the consumer. Usually, the *seller* is due the income from these orders. Len recommends that a final accounting of the total completed work be made a day or two before the sale. The buyer, in most cases, will purchase these accounts for 70-80% *of the balance due,* excluding any orders sitting on the shelf for over 4-6 months. Items, that have remained unclaimed for over six months, would be significantly discounted.

Finished orders that have been delivered—If any balance is still outstanding, the income from these orders are due the seller.

Orders still at the lab or album company—Today, many photographers get most, if not all of the money prior to the order going into production (a practice I highly recommend). Since the seller has already collected the clients' money, there may not be enough money left over for the buyer to cover the cost of actually fulfilling the order. Consequently, adjustments need to be made by the buyer to the seller. The same is true for orders that have been returned from the lab but have yet to be assembled.

Previews—This refers to previews that have been delivered to the client but no order has been made. If the seller has collected only the sitting fee, the negatives and subsequent sales will belong to the buyer. The buyer should pay particular attention to weddings and social events. For example, suppose you have 30 weddings on the books—some partially completed, others yet to be photographed. It's not uncommon for a photographer to have a retainer of $1,000 or more. If the seller kept the money, the buyer would do all the work and have nothing to show for it. In determining the purchase price, take deposits into consideration. Arrangements regarding preview and subsequent orders must be addressed prior to the purchase and sale agreement.

Whatever the price may be, Len recommends placing 10-15% of the purchase price into escrow for unplanned expenses and surprises—a wise practice for anyone who purchases a studio.

OTHER CONSIDERATIONS

Len offers the following advice to anyone contemplating the purchase or sale of a photography studio:

Rent/Lease—Typically rent is 5-10% of a studio's gross sales. Before the sale, check on the number of years remaining, option(s) for renewal, possible extensions, and/or option to purchase.

The Lucrative Photographer

Location—This is particularly important if you are purchasing a studio that is located in the seller's home. Other considerations: Is the studio on street level or on a second or third floor? Are there many vacant stores in the area? Is there ample room for parking or expansion?

Financial Statements—Try to obtain the last seven years of financial records with particular attention to the last three years. (Ask to see the seller's Federal Tax Returns.) Len says to disregard statements made by the seller who says he/she makes more than what is shown on the financial statements. Len notes that some studios with high gross sales may not generate a lot in the way of profit. Maybe their prices are too low, their rent is too high, or the studio was not well run. In doing your due diligence prior to the sale, if you encounter a studio such as this, you must understand that you will need to make major changes in the way the studio operates, or the studio will not prosper. You may want to use the results of my survey on photographers' business practices as a reference point for how your business (if you're selling) or the potential business (if you're buying) compares to studios in general. Other financial considerations:

- Make sure your lawyer and accountant review all documents and records before you enter into a Purchase and Sale Agreement
- Make sure all taxes due are current and that there are no liens on the equipment or the business.
- Make sure there are no pending lawsuits against the studio.

Protecting Your Assets

Goodwill—Earlier we talked about tangible assets such as camera equipment and inventory. Goodwill is an intangible asset. Goodwill is the value a buyer places on the future earning power of a studio. In fact, that is really why you are buying a studio versus starting one from scratch, brand name recognition. While goodwill can be worth 20-25% (or more) of the selling price, you need to check with your accountant on how to handle goodwill in the sale of a business.

Depreciation—Most people, according to Len, do not realize the importance of depreciation. Depreciation is a tax credit on assets you have purchased that extends over a period of time (the "useful life" of the asset). While depreciation is used as a deduction on your taxes, it is not an out-of-pocket expense.

Depreciation is particularly important if you apply to the bank for a loan (to purchase a studio for example). As noted earlier, most banks don't expect you to use your salary to repay the loan; they expect payment to come from your studio's net profit *plus* depreciation. If the bank does not believe there is sufficient cash flow to repay the loan, they will refuse to grant the loan in the first place. The good news according to Len, is when you purchase a studio, you will have a large base for tax credits due to the advantage of depreciation.

Let's go back to our original example. The monthly business mortgage payment is $1,586. Suppose your monthly depreciation expense is $1,200 (for example purposes only). If, after depreciation, your studio profit was $1,200 per month, you may think you are well below the $2,400 in income the bank requires.

However, banks understand that depreciation is a non-cash accounting expense and will add the depreciation amount back into income, giving you the necessary $2,400 income level.

Contracts—Besides goodwill, another reason for purchasing a studio outright is the existing contracts the studio has secured. As with any legal document, you should have them reviewed by your attorney. From a business point of view, you should determine what is required to fulfill the contracts. Are rebates required? How many jobs are on the books and how much has been pre-paid?

Contracts with the Seller—You should determine how long (if at all) the seller plans to remain in the business after the sale to help make the transition easier. You should also discuss whether or not the seller plans to continue in professional photography, on his/her own after the sale. Either way you will want the seller to establish a non-compete clause that will restrict or prohibit the seller from opening or buying another studio within 5-10 years from the date of the sale and/or within a specified radius of the studio.

Seek advice—Everyone emphasized the importance of getting expert advice. Before purchasing a studio you should have all documents reviewed by your accountant, lawyer, and banker. Investing in their services before the sale can save you countless dollars and heartache.

HOW MUCH IS A STUDIO WORTH?

Annual Gross Sales (A)	$_____
Average Gross Sales last three years	$_____
Total fair market values of tangible assets (B)	$_____
Value of Studio's Goodwill	$_____
Studio Profit (C)(after salary and expenses)	$_____

Business Evaluation Methods

Percentage of Sales
Gross Sales times 60-65% (A*.60) $ _____

Tangible Assets
Tangible assets times 2 (B*2) $ _____

Multiple of Net Earnings
True net income times 3 (C*3) $ _____

Adjustments:
Work-In-Progress $ _____
Depreciation $ _____
Goodwill $ _____

Negotiated Selling Price $ _____

Purchasing Considerations
Monthly Business Mortgage Payment $ _____
Monthly Studio Profit (before depreciation) $ _____
Net difference $ _____
(Studio Profit should be 1.4 to 1.5 times the Business Mortgage Payment. To obtain a loan. If difference is negative, where will money come from?)

Return On Investment
Yearly Studio Profit/Annual Gross Sales   _____ %
Rate of Return if Money was Invested   _____ %
Number of years to recover investment   _____
(Studio rate of return should be at least equal to investment rate of return in the long run)

In determining a business' worth, consider using all three-valuation methods. For example, a business that has gross sales of $150,000 may not have any real profit left over after the owner pays his or her salary. In

254

this instance all you are really buying is the equipment, contracts on the books, and some amount of goodwill.

WHO FINANCES THE SALE?

I would like to issue a word of caution. Some owners may be tempted to finance the sale of their studio themselves. In which case the buyer of the studio pays the seller a monthly installment, instead of financing the sale through a bank. The risk to the seller is that the buyer will not succeed. If this happens, as a seller, you may end up losing money, or having to take back the studio you thought you already sold. Many large companies have faced severe financial hardship and even failure because of poor credit decisions they made with their clients. If the potential borrower cannot obtain financing from a bank, it is usually for a very good reason. Before you proceed, seek the council of qualified professionals and make sure it is in your best interest and you are well compensated for the added risk.

Note: The Federal Government under the Small Business Administration (SBA) offers special lending programs. To view the latest programs and lending requirements visit their website at www.sba.gov.

WHAT IF I DON'T PLAN ON SELLING?

Even if you don't plan to sell your studio, I recommend you periodically establish your business' worth. In many ways, this is the true measure of how lucrative you really are. Earlier I used the example of looking at a sale as if you were an investor. All too often, photographers think of salary and studio profit as one in the same; they are not. Determining your studio's worth illustrates the point. If you plan on selling the business in the future, assessing the value of your business today will give you a basis for where you need to go in order to secure the price you want, when you want it. Either way, valuing your business on a regular basis is a good reality check on where you stand today.

SUMMARY

Many factors will determine the success or failure of a newly purchased photography studio. The new owner needs to have sufficient business, marketing and photographic skills to ensure the continued success of the studio. But even before taking over he or she needs to know what is ahead. Consider Len and Jack's recommendation and seek professional advice before entering any agreement.

GOVERNMENT
The US Small Business Administration (SBA)— www.sba.gov (There are local offices in each state.)

ASSOCIATIONS:
*The Professional Photographers of America—*229 Peachtree Street NE, Suite 2200 International Tower, Atlanta, Georgia 30303-1608, 404-522-8600, www.ppa-world.org

Wedding and Portrait Photographers International— 1312 Lincoln Blvd., Santa Monica, California 90401-2003, 310-451-0090, www.wppi-online.com

LEGAL:
Ronald M. Rubin, Rubin and Zimmerman, PC,
9725 E. Hampden, #330 Denver, CO 80231, Tel:
303-306-6191, Fax: 303-306-7603, ron@rzpc.com

SOFTWARE
Dantz Development Corporation—4 Orinda Way,
Bldg. C, Orinda, California 94563, 925-253-3000,
www.dantz.com

Symantec Corp., 20330 Stevens Creek Blvd.,
Cupertino, California 95014, 408-253-9600,
www.symantec.com

McAfee.com—McAfee.com, 3965 Freedom Circle,
Santa Clara, California 95054, 408-572-1500,
www.mcafee.com

Quicken—Intuit, Inc., 2535 Garcia Avenue,
Mountain View, California 94043, 800-446-8848,
www.intuit.com

Microsoft Money— Microsoft Corp., One Microsoft
Way, Redmond, Washington, 98052-6399, 425-882-
8080, www.microsoft.com

CONSULTANTS/COMPNANIES
Contact your local bank, CPA, and Attorney to assist
you with your sale or purchase.

Protecting Your Assets

Baystate Financial Services—Jim Wolfson, CFP, ChFC, CLU, 1 Exeter Plz Ste 1400, Boston, Massachusetts 02116-2848, (617) 585-4594, jwolfson@boston-bfs.nefn.com, http://www.baystatefinancial.com

HDH Associates (Howard Hillman)—5 Commonwealth Road, Natick, Massachusetts 01760-1526, 508-650-9444, hdh@lanprobus.com

PC Software & Hardware Repair (Steve Sotsky)—25 Driscoll Drive, Framingham, Massachusetts 01701-3475, 508-877-4578, SandHAssoc@AOL.com

Aronson Insurance, Aronson Insurance, Newton, MA 617-965-3030

Seabury & Smith-Park Ridge, PO Box 4196, Carol Stream, IL 60197-4196, 800-503-9227

Epilogue

Upon reflection, I believe that to be truly lucrative one must possess six key traits:

LUCRATIVE BUSINESS TRAITS
- Positive mental attitude
- Professionalism
- Consistency in their work and attitude
- Customer service
- Treating their profession a business practices
- Having balance in their life

POSITIVE MENTAL ATTITUDE[43]

The chemistry between artist and client is vital. No one wants a grouchy photographer. Unfortunately for some photographers, their initial enthusiasm for the business fades and cynicism and negative thoughts begin to take over.

I can't recall a single person I consider to be successful, who doesn't have a positive mental attitude. Each of them has an enthusiasm that is infectious. Their positive outlook on life instills confidence and makes for a more positive buying experience. Think back on what made you initially

---

[43]Two great resources on this topic are *Think and Grow Rich*, Napoleon Hill and *Success Through a Positive Mental Attitude*, W. Clement Stone

become a photographer. Grab onto to that feeling and share it with your customers.

PROFESSIONALISM

Whether it's how you dress, answer the telephone, deliver your photography, or present your price lists, each customer contact is a reflection of you and your studio. Professionalism instills respect, and respect helps you command the prices you deserve. Lucrative businesses strive to always show off their best.

CONSISTENCY

How long would you use a film if one roll were a stop under and the next a stop over with no way of predicting what the end result would be? Could you use a lab if you never knew how long it would take for them to print your order?

It is human nature to desire predictable results. Look at McDonalds or Pizza Hut. Neither company professes to offer the best product. Yet people go there because they know in advance what to expect.

The importance of consistency extends beyond simply the quality of your product or service. How often would you shop at a store if the salesperson had a Jeckle and Hyde personality?

These examples illustrate why lucrative businesses are fanatical about the quality of what they offer and who they hire to work with the public. They know that inconsistency is one of the quickest ways to send clients to the competition.

The Lucrative Photographer

CUSTOMER SERVICE

I can't overstate the importance of treating your clients with reverence. The true measure of your customer service is how you handle problems. As noted earlier, for every $1 you spend in adequately addressing customer problems, you get $2 back in return. The top companies do whatever it takes to make sure clients always leave happy.

TREAT YOUR STUDIO AS A BUSINESS

If you simply enjoy creating pretty images for fun you have a hobby. On the other hand, if you charge clients for your photographic skills, you are operating a business. From the publics' point-of-view, it doesn't matter whether photography is your full-time profession or simply a part-time indulgence.

This is an important distinction. Once you decide to go from amateur to professional, you owe it to yourself and your colleagues to treat your business as a business. Lucrative photographers are not bashful about making a fair profit and neither should you.

HAVE BALANCE

Being a lucrative photographer is not about being full-time or part-time, it is not about what style of photography you practice, or which end of the market you serve. Nor is it about selling pieces of paper, albums, wall prints, or frames. To be lucrative you need to have balance. There is more to life than work. Remember to stop every now and then to enjoy life.

I wish you a long and lucrative career.

About The Author

Mark Till, Cr. Photog., is one of the country's leading authorities on helping photographers operate a lucrative business. He is the author of *The Lucrative Photographer: How to Become Indispensable To Your Clients, Maximize Your Profitability, and Regain Your Personal Life.* Mark is a frequent lecturer across the country and when he is not speaking, consults one on one with professional photographers. Mark offers onsite classes, seminars and lectures and programs via the telephone. Mark Till Consulting was created in response to repeated requests from fellow photographers regarding help in running their business. Mark is also a featured magazine columnist throughout the US and Canada.

Mark continues to own Till Photography, in Natick, MA along with his wife Laura, specializing in photographing weddings and social events. Their commitment to photographic quality and customer service has made him one of the Boston area's premier wedding photographers.

If you found this book helpful and would like more information about other products, professional services, private and group consultations, and seminars offered by Mark Till Consulting, call (508) 655-9595 or fax (561) 673-8008 or e-mail mark@marktill.com or write Mark D. Till, Cr. Photog., *Mark Till Consulting*, Six Surrey Lane, Natick, Massachusetts 01760-3335.

Appendix

☞ Break-Even Worksheet
☞ Business Plan Outline
☞ Twelve Steps To A Better Website
☞ Asset Inventory Worksheet

Appendix

Break-Even Worksheet

EMPLOYEE BENEFITS[44]

Owner's Compensation
    Salary $_____
    Medical Insurance $_____
    Dental Insurance $_____
    Disability Insurance $_____
    Retirement Plan $_____
    Other $_____
(1) Total Owner's Compensation $_____

Employee Compensation
    Salary $_____
    Medical Insurance $_____
    Dental Insurance $_____
    Disability Insurance $_____
    Retirement Plan $_____
    Other $_____
(2) Total Employee Compensation $_____

MARKETING

    Print Ads $_____
    Web page/Internet $_____
    Brochures $_____
    Direct Mail $_____
    Newsletters $_____
    Client Appreciation $_____
    Networking $_____
    Other $_____
(3) Total Marketing $_____

ADMINISTRATION

    Loan Payments $_____
    Automotive $_____
    Repairs & Maintenance $_____

[44] Total benefits are approximately 40% of salary.

The Lucrative Photographer

Fees/Charges $ _____
Education $ _____
Insurance $ _____
Office Supplies $ _____
Postage $ _____
Professional Services $ _____
Telephone $ _____
Entertainment $ _____
(4) Administration Expense $ _____

OVERHEAD
Rent/Mortgage $ _____
Utilities $ _____
Other $ _____
(5) Total Employee Compensation $ _____

NON-CAPITAL EQUIPMENT PURCHASE
Camera $ _____
Office $ _____
Computer $ _____
Other $ _____
(6) Total Marketing $ _____

DEPRECIATION
(7) Total Depreciation Expense $ _____

NON-OPERATING EXPENSES
Loan Interest $ _____
Other $ _____
(8) Total Non-Operating Expense $ _____

FIXED EXPENSE SUMMARY
(1) Owner's Compensation $ _____
(2) Employee Compensation $ _____
(3) Marketing $ _____
(4) Administration $ _____
(5) Overhead $ _____
(6) Non-Capital Equipment $ _____
(7) Depreciation $ _____

Appendix

(8) Non-Balance Sheet Expenses $_____

(9) Total Fixed Expenses[45] $_____

(10) Cost of Goods Sold (%of Sales   _____ %

BREAK-EVEN FORMULA: FIXED EXPENSES/(1-CGS)

(11) Break-Even Sales Total $_____

(12) Profit (10-15% of sales (above) $_____

(13) Total Break-Even Sales $_____

BREAK-EVEN SALES BY PRODUCT MIX
Break-Even Sales Mix (Percentage)[46]
    Product 1 _____   _____ %
    Product 2 _____   _____ %
    Product 3 _____   _____ %

Break-Even Sales Mix (Number)[47]
    Product 1 _____   _____
    Product 2 _____   _____
    Product 3 _____   _____

Break-Even Sales Mix (Dollar Amount)[48]
    Product 1 _____   _____ %
    Product 2 _____   _____ %
    Product 3 _____   _____ %

---

[45] Consult your accountant or tax preparer for treatment and allocation of all expenses.

[46] What percentage of your business do you want each product/service to be, as a percentage of sales.

[47] How many sittings do you want to do for each product/service/

[48] Multiply break-even sales by product percentage and divide by the total number of sessions you plan to do.

The Lucrative Photographer

Business Plan Outline

GENERAL COMPANY DESCRIPTION

Provide a perspective of your industry and how your business fits into the total picture.

1. Profile of your current business situation
2. Profile of your specific market
3. Anticipated challenges and responses

OBJECTIVES

1. Do you plan to stay a one-person shop, or do you plan to build a larger company with multiple photographers? (Explain)
2. Do you plan to pass the ownership of your studio down to your children or other family members?
3. What do expect to generate in profits in the next five years?
4. In order to achieve your goals, will you have to borrow money? If yes, how much and what method of financing will you use?
5. What are your sales projections for the next five years?

PRODUCTS/SERVICES

1. Product/Service description—describe the products and services you plan to offer
2. Added value—what are the added-value features of your specific products/services. What makes them unique?

Appendix

3. Product life-cycle—buying frequency, warrantee/guarantee, customer lifecycle, etc.
4. Trademarks/copyright

MARKET ANALYSIS
1. Market definitions
2. Strengths and weaknesses
3. Customer profile
4. Competition

MARKETING AND SALES STRATEGY
1. Marketing plan
2. Sales tactics
3. USP
4. Marketing objectives
5. Ads and promotions

FINANCIAL PLANNING & ASSET PROTECTION
1. Retirement objectives
2. Insurance coverage
3. Long-term financial objectives
4. Data protection
5. Legal Protection

FINANCIAL PROJECTIONS
1. Budget
2. P&L
3. Balance Sheet
4. Break-even analysis
5. Projections (3-5 years)

Twelve Steps To A Better Website

STEP #1: DETERMINE YOUR OBJECTIVES

Make a list of everything you would like your website to do for your business. It will obviously serve as a marketing piece, probably display your portfolio, but are there other services or day-to-day business tasks that could be handled via the website? Think about your workflow and explore creative ideas that will enable your website to add extra value and convenience for you and your customers. Let your ideas run rampant now and worry about how to implement them later.

STEP #2: CHART YOUR COURSE

Map out your website before you begin production by creating a flowchart that illustrates how the site will be organized. This is a good exercise even if you are planning on hiring a professional web developer to build your site, as it will provide them with a clear schematic of your objectives from the outset. The site map will also serve to solidify your ideas and provide a model for what the visitor's experience will be. When you're finished with your site map set it aside for a day or two, then come back and revisit it from a user's perspective. Does the information flow well? Is the content well organized? Will everything be easy to find? At this point it's also a good idea to share your site map with a friend or two to get their feedback, then make any necessary tweaks to make it as user-friendly as possible.

Appendix

Now that you have your site map, review it again from your own perspective. Have you created a monster? Is there a lot of content that will require weekly or monthly maintenance? Remember, once the site is up and running it will be your responsibility to keep it up-to-date, either by doing it yourself or paying someone else to do it. Either way, content demanding regular maintenance will require a long-term commitment involving time and/or money to feed the beast. Make sure that your website plans are meeting your objectives but not creating another full-time job for yourself; pare away any unnecessary content that may cause headaches for you later on.

STEP #3: SHOP THE COMPETITION
With your site map in-hand, spend some time surfing the web to see what your competition is up to. View these sites with an eye for both content and design; getting a good look at the competition may even spark some additional ideas you hadn't thought of. Are they reaching the same objectives you will be striving for? What improvements could you make for your site? What about design— what do you feel works and what doesn't? Are the sites easy to navigate or are they cumbersome? Bookmark sites you like as well as sites that you don't like; this will serve as good reference material when you're ready to begin production (even if you're hiring a web developer, it's great to give them examples of your likes and dislikes before they get started).

STEP #4: OBTAIN REAL ESTATE FOR YOUR WEBSITE
Unless you have your own server you'll need to open a web hosting account where your website will reside.

You will also want to register your own unique domain name (www.yourname.com) with VeriSign (the company responsible for registering these names). This may seem obvious, but it's best to get this all squared away sooner than later so you can secure the domain name you want and also have a place to test the site while it's under construction. There are so many hosting companies with different packages available that choosing one can get quite complicated. Make a list of all the features your site will need (like mail forwarding, streaming video, mailing list capabilities, etc.) so you'll have a checklist in-hand when you begin shopping for a service provider. This will make it much easier to compare the different packages available once you become immersed in the quagmire of offerings. Also take into consideration what kind of customer service is available (call or contact them via email with a question to test them out) and whether or not they offer any nice convenience features (like web-based control panels to manage different aspects of your account).

STEP #5: EXPLORE APPLICATION SERVICE PROVIDERS
Remember back in Step 1 when I mentioned you could worry about implementing your great ideas later on? That's where Application Service Providers come in. ASP's are third party services you can buy into to add additional functionality to your website at a fraction of the cost that it would take to develop the same functionality on your own. For example, if you want to offer a feature that would allow your clients to view proofs online and order prints directly from your website, you can do so via a service such as PhotosAtMyDoor. By using their service you'll be able

Appendix

to add the functionality you want for a reasonable monthly fee — and you won't have to build it from scratch (which would be a very costly venture). There are all kinds of third-party applications available—some of them are even free. It's just a matter of doing the research—so web developers, start your search engines.

STEP #6: CREATE A USER-FRIENDLY DESIGN

Now that you've determined what your content is going to be it's time to design what your website will look like. At this point you might want to consider hiring a web developer to get you from point A to point B. Or, if you're in a do-it-yourself frame of mind, you can take on the project yourself. Either way, use your other marketing materials as a starting point to establish color palettes, typefaces, etc. (it's always a good idea to keep all of your marketing materials consistent). Revisit some of the sites you liked earlier, as well as other sites you frequently visit, and pay close attention of what makes them appealing or easy to use then try to apply these same principles to your own design. Create a page framework or template that will be used for every page in your website. This framework should include your logo, navigation buttons for all items on your site map, and a footer containing general contact info, an email link, and maybe some copyright information. Remember, people won't always be entering your website via the home page, so make sure they'll know who you are no matter what page they land on. Create your template design in a painting or drawing program (such as Photoshop) it will allow you more creative freedom than if you jump straight to HTML and it can also serve as the

274

basis for the graphics prep you'll need to do later when you prepare your pages. To ensure your page will be fully viewable on most computer monitors without the need to scroll left and right, keep the width of your template 795 pixels or less.

STEP #7: GET TO KNOW THE CODE

Once you have your design ready you'll need to create a template in HTML. HTML, or Hypertext Markup Language, is the language used to create web pages; it's basically a text-based description that tells the web browser (like Netscape or Internet Explorer) what and where everything is on a page. HTML is relatively easy to learn and your favorite bookstore is probably stocked with countless tomes on the subject. All you need is knowledge of the code and a basic text editor to write HTML, and there are many good shareware applications available that make the process much easier. There are also more expensive commercial applications available (such as Macromedia's DreamWeaver™) that work like a page layout program, allowing you to place objects and text on a page while it writes the HTML code in the background. Regardless of what you use you'll want to familiarize yourself with the finer points of HTML coding, as you'll find that even the code generated by visual-based HTML editors often needs tweaking. There are many online resources and tutorials available for learning the HTML language (I have listed a few below). You can also look under the hood of websites you like by selecting "Page Source" under the "View" menu of your browser; this will display the HTML written for the page and allow you to see how other HTML coders approach different situations.

HTML TUTORIALS AND
RESOURCES FOR WEBSITE DEVELOPMENT

HTML Made Really Easy
http://www.jmarshall.com/easy/html/

Worldwide Web Consortium
http://www.w3.org/

Creating Killer Websites
http://www.killersites.com

Web Monkey
http://www.webmonkey.com

STEP #8: FAMILIARIZE YOURSELF WITH IMAGE FORMATS

If you're building the website yourself, it's important to understand the two file formats used for images on the web: GIF and JPEG. GIFs are most appropriate for graphic images (logos, buttons, etc.) while JPEGs work best for photographic type images. Choosing the right file format when saving each of your images can dramatically optimize the loading time of your pages— photos look better as JPEGs and load up to three times faster than if they were saved as a GIF, and the inverse can also be true for graphic images. Experiment with both file types when creating your images, and be aware of the difference in file sizes before incorporating the images into your pages.

STEP #9: CREATE A GOOD FIRST IMPRESSION

Now that you have a page template you can begin creating your home page. The goal of your home page should be to inform visitors what your business is all about in a matter of seconds. Be sure to include a company mission statement and consider providing a content overview to let visitors know what they'll find behind each button.

STEP: 10: WHAT YOU SEE MAY NOT BE WHAT OTHERS GET

Whether you take on the HTML coding yourself or hire a professional to do the work, make sure you check your web pages on both Netscape and Internet Explorer before giving them your final blessing. The two most commonly used web browsers interpret HTML code a slightly different from one another and it's good practice to make sure everybody will be seeing close to the same thing no matter which browser they use. Also, the font you choose for the text on your pages should be a standard font that is found on most computer systems, such as Helvetica, Times New Roman, and Ariel. You may find text size differentials from browser to browser, but by previewing the page in different browsers you can make adjustments that will make it display nicely in any situation.

STEP #11: BE CONSISTENT AND CLEAN

Don't stray from your template when you're building your site. Consistency is the key to a user-friendly experience for your visitors and you should avoid disorienting them by introducing different design or navigation elements in your template from page-to-page. Avoid using gratuitous effects (animation, java tricks, etc.) unless they directly contribute to the content of the page.

STEP #12: FOCUS ON YOUR CONTENT, NOT YOUR SEARCH ENGINE RANKING

Don't be more concerned with your site's ranking on the search engines than you are with its actual content. The fact of the matter is that content is the most important attribute that will ultimately determine how high your site is ranked on the search engines. Meta-tag keywords and descriptions are important to include in your HTML code, but don't consider them a substitute for well-produced content.

RESOURCES

CONSULTANTS

Stephen Simon Multimedia Design, Stephen Simon, 42 Kent Street, #2, Brookline, Massachusetts 02445, (781) 730-5766, ssimon@world.std.com.

Asset Inventory

Most businesses perform an inventory of the company's assets on an annual basis. You will need to perform in inventory for several reasons. First, many cities and towns assess a property tax on a business's assets. Your inventory is used to determine your tax liability. Second, if you need to borrow money, your bank may look to your business's assets as collateral for the loan. The third reason is insurance. You need to identify those assets you wish to insure in case of loss or theft. Lack of a detailed asset listing could have adverse effect on your ability to recover from a loss. And finally, it is a sound business practice to determine your company's net worth each year as an indication of your company's financial strength.

It is also a good idea to keep a copy of your company's assets in a safe place, away from the business location, such as a safe deposit box. Many insurance companies recommend you include photographs or video of the assets to support your paperwork. (This is also a good idea for you personal possessions as well.)

To perform your asset inventory, you will need to gather the following information:

* Date of purchase
* Description of the asset
* Serial numbers (if applicable)

* Purchase amount
* Current market value
* Replacement cost

The market value is what you city or town will use to assess the property tax. The value does not have to be exact, but it should be "reasonable" in case you are ever audited. The replacement cost is optional, but I recommend it because in many instances, this is the value you will use for your insurance policy.

While many accounting and studio management programs track company assets, I personally keep my inventory on an excel spreadsheet which makes it easy to update each year. The choice is yours, but it is a good idea to check with your accountant to see which method they prefer.

Below is a sample asset inventory. Use this model as is or adapt it for your own personal situation.[49] I recommend using a spreadsheet like Microsoft Excel. Subtotal each page to make compiling totals easier.

ASSET INVENTORY WORKSHEET

Purchase Date	Serial #	Asset Description	Purchase Price	Market Value	Replacement Cost
1/1/02	54895	Bronica SQ-Ai Body	$950	$375	$1,200
1/1/02	12345	80mm 2.8 Lens	$650	$500	$800

[49] *Note*: market value is what the equipment is worth today if you were to sell it on the open market. Replacement cost is what you would need to pay to replace the equipment if it was lost or damaged beyond repair..